Resettling
Retarded Adults in a
Managed Community

Arnold Birenbaum
Samuel Seiffer
foreword by
Stephen A. Richardson

The Praeger Special Studies program—utilizing the most modern and efficient book production techniques and a selective worldwide distribution network—makes available to the academic, government, and business communities significant, timely research in U.S. and international economic, social, and political development.

Resettling
Retarded Adults in a
Managed Community

PRAEGER SPECIAL STUDIES IN U.S. ECONOMIC, SOCIAL, AND POLITICAL ISSUES

Praeger Publishers   New York   Washington   London

Library of Congress Cataloging in Publication Data

Birenbaum, Arnold.
    Resettling retarded adults in a managed community.

    (Praeger special studies in U.S. economic, social,
and political issues)
    Includes index.
    1. Mentally handicapped—Institutional care—New
York (City)   2.   Mentally handicapped—Rehabilitation—
New York (City)   I. Seiffer, Samuel, joint author.
II. Title. [DNLM: 1. Mental retardation—Rehabilitation.
2. Therapeutic community.   3. Residential facilities—
U.S. WM30 B618r]
HV3006.N69B57   362.3   75-19765
ISBN 0-275-55520-8

PRAEGER PUBLISHERS
111 Fourth Avenue, New York, N.Y. 10003, U.S.A.

Published in the United States of America in 1976
by Praeger Publishers, Inc.

Printed in the United States of America

The limited economic, social, and human resources of the modern family have made public and private social agencies an indispensable and essential source of services for those who are severely mentally handicapped. Many forms of services are possible for these agencies, including residential institutions. The dominant form of mental retardation service which emerged at the end of the nineteenth century was continuous care in large isolated institutions. There are, of course, other existing facilities that may not require the removal of the retarded person from his home; neighborhood day care, for example, can take responsibility for supervision during working hours, and homemakers can provide a respite when parents are needed or wish to be outside the home.

Increasingly, parents and professionals have recommended the development of small residential units within communities so that mentally retarded persons can remain near their families. These residential units utilize many of the existing community resources for health, education, and vocational services and provide for short term as well as long term residential needs. The experience gained with hostels, small homes, foster care arrangements, and apartment living in Sweden, Denmark, and England (Kushlick 1975), has led to the planning of similar facilities in the United States.

There are two major kinds of living arrangements which mentally retarded persons have experienced. First, there are individuals who have been placed in large and isolated traditional institutions for the retarded—with many spending such large portions of their lives in such settings that these facilities often become the only places they know. Second, there are people who have remained at home, and whose families have, in some cases, been given supplementary help from outside agencies. If the large institutions are phased out, the number of mentally retarded people in the first group will diminish and eventually disappear. It is essential, however, in planning programs for small residential facilities, to recognize that the mentally retarded people who have lived for long periods in large institutions will have very different experiences, training, and behavior compared to those who have lived with their families.

Stephen A. Richardson, Ph.D., is Professor of Pediatrics and Community Health at the Albert Einstein College of Medicine.

This book is about mentally retarded persons coming out of traditional institutions. It concerns mentally retarded adults who, after spending many years in large institutions, moved to a small residence located in the community from which they originally came. The first two years of their lives in the smaller community residence are described. It is particularly important to have studies of this initial period. Traditional mental retardation institutions have been in existence for almost one hundred years and a great deal of experience has been gained with this form of care. These institutions have been the subject of many studies which have evaluated both the operation of such facilities and their effect on the lives of the residents. In part, the results of these studies have provided the impetus for alternative forms of residential care, and for training programs to help some residents prepare for a life outside of residential institutions.

Presently, pioneering efforts in residential care are moving forward with enthusiasm. It is theorized that new forms of care in or near the communities in which the families of the mentally retarded live, will be more humane and will provide an environment where the capacities of the mentally retarded can better be developed. There is some empirical evidence to support these beliefs but more studies are needed. As with most innovations and changes in arranging human affairs, there are, in addition to intended consequences, also unintended consequences which can be either assets or liabilities to the original objectives for which the changes were planned. Unfortunately many of the changes in the field of mental retardation are put into effect hastily and in response to intense political pressures, without any systematic attempt either to describe or evaluate the changes. Where information about change is obtained it is often from those responsible for it, who cannot be in an objective position to judge the effects of what they do. The authors of this book acted independently of those responsible for establishing and running the small residence discussed here, and this is a great advantage.

When long established social programs become subject to change and possible termination, vested interests in the established programs lead to opposition to change, greatly increasing the difficulty of accomplishing innovations. To determine whether or not there are sound reasons for the opposition, it is essential to have pilot programs that test the effects of the changes on those served. The results of these studies engender debate which includes evidence and conclusions from the systematic evaluation of the pilot experience.

In assessing the level of functioning of adults who are severely mentally retarded, and who have spent long periods of their lives in large isolated institutions, it is not possible to determine how much functional impairment one can attribute to the congenital defect or biologic damage, or how much one can attribute to the individual's experiences. Small community residences, together with a variety of other community services, give a very different set of social experiences which can provide better opportunity for the optimal development of the retarded. This makes possible the study of the effects of varying forms of socialization on the mentally retarded.

The term mental retardation, even with the qualification of moderate or severe, encompasses a wide variety of people with vastly different needs. It is easy to slip into a pattern of thinking where all the retarded are considered as a relatively homogeneous group and can thus receive roughly the same treatment, with relatively little individual variation in daily programs. This has led to management practices in institutions, well described by King, Raynes, and Tizard (1971), which include rigidity of routine, block treatment, depersonalization, and social distance between staff and residents. It is hoped that small residential facilities linked to a network of community services will provide an organization of services, permitting greater range and flexibility in order to meet the multiple and varied needs of the mentally retarded and their families.

The description of the experiences of adults who were moved from large residential institutions to small residences set in the community provides a valuable case study from which the reader can learn much. The value of the study will be increased if further studies are made and become available so that the results can be compared across studies.

REFERENCES

King, John, Norma Raynes, and Jack Tizard
  1971   Patterns of Residential Care. London: Routledge, Kegan
          Paul.
Kushlick, A.
  1975   "Epidemiology and evaluation of services for the men-
          tally handicapped," in M. Begab and S. A. Richardson,
          editors, The Mentally Retarded and Society. Baltimore:
          University Park Press.

This investigation was made possible by the generous Core Grant from the National Institute of Child Health and Human Development to the Rose F. Kennedy Center for Research in Mental Retardation and Human Development of Albert Einstein College of Medicine. Professor Stephen Richardson, Director of the Social Ecology Research Unit provided much encouragement and useful criticism throughout the course of our research and the preparation of this report.

Many people employed by various agencies in the field of mental retardation were extremely helpful and encouraging by providing access to their clients and other agencies involved in the creation of the program for the resettlement of mentally retarded adults. At a time when services for the mentally retarded as well as other groups of handicapped persons were under great criticism, a number of people persisted in defining research as an important part of their commitment to the development of services for the mentally retarded in the community. It is to their credit that they at no time attempted to interfere with our goal of ascertaining the facts and reporting the resettlement experience with the objectivity such an undertaking requires. Specifically, we wish to thank: Dr. Herbert Cohen, Dr. David Kligler, Dr. Howard Demb, Mr. Fred Markowitz, Mr. Ernest Koller, Mr. David Woogin, Mr. Maurice Halefi, Mr. Thomas Scharff, Ms. Mary Ann Dee and Dr. Max Dubrow.

Ms. Sarah Goldsmith deserves special thanks. Her personal involvement in the well-being of the resettled mentally retarded adults contributed greatly to her success in interviewing the women of Gatewood. Ms. Wendy Walker was also extremely helpful during the first wave of interviews.

Dr. Helene Levens Lipton, Dr. Bonnie Svarstad, Dr. Helen Abramowicz, Ms. Helene Koller, and Ms. Ellen Grabie, our colleagues at the Social Ecology Research Unit during the course of the study, were continuously helpful and supportive. Dr. Robert Friis generously provided continuous consultation as we prepared the tabular presentation of our data. We also wish to acknowledge efforts of Sylvia Friberg, Madeline Treat, Elaine Cranston and Barbara Yula, who patiently typed the various drafts of the manuscript. The Columbia University Computer Center aided us greatly by making their facilities available for the processing of our data.

Finally, and most importantly, we wish to publicly thank the men and women who told us about the way they lived in state schools and in the community. In order to maintain the anonymity of the respondents we cannot mention their names. We hope that this study will assist them and other mentally retarded persons to live more freely, experience the full range of joy and sadness possible for human beings, and to be able to make their contribution to the common weal.

Page

LIST OF TABLES

A man in his early thirties lives in a large city. At seven A.M. the alarm rings in his room. His roommate has long since gone to work. After turning off the alarm, he gets out of bed, washes, shaves, brushes his teeth, and has his breakfast. He gets his sandwich for lunch and meets a fellow worker with whom he travels by bus to his shop. At the end of the work day they return home together. Later with his dinner companions, he discusses the events of the day and his plans for the weekend. After dinner, he watches television, has a snack, and talks to a friend about the program on the screen. After saying goodnight, he goes off to his room where he finds his roommate already asleep. Tomorrow, he thinks, they will have to clean up their room. He turns on the radio very softly, so as not to disturb his roommate, in order to relax before going to sleep. He sets his alarm clock so that he will wake up at seven o'clock and be able to arrive at work by the required time. Tomorrow is payday and he thinks about what he will do with the money. Perhaps he will go to the new James Bond movie at the local theater.

This composite picture of a day in the life of an ordinary member of the community is not very astonishing. It is a life of normal appearances and conventional activities. Nothing much happens during this typical day but less than two years ago this mentally retarded adult was a patient in a residential state school in a rural area, a place where he had lived since the age of sixteen. At the school he spent much of his time waiting for meals, watching television or wielding a mop in the dormitory which he shared with seventy-nine other men. Despite an I.Q. of 51, after eighteen years of institutional living this man has been resettled at a community residence, where, with some help, he is expected to utilize community resources for vocational rehabilitation, recreation, and health services. Only in the last few years have patients from state schools in the United States been able to leave these large and isolated residential institutions in any numbers. This is the story of what happened to some former patients from state schools; the story of their return to society.

The large and isolated institution for the mentally retarded has recently become the subject of investigative reporting (Rivera 1972) and class action suits on behalf of residents at these facilities (Goodman 1974). Lacking social stimulation and privacy, persons in these environments become apathetic and acquire an institutional demeanor, while overcrowded conditions produce serious neglect of basic care (Blatt 1974). Consequently, federal district courts have ruled that

some institutions could not provide a safe and wholesome environment
for so many people, and state agencies in charge of these facilities
were ordered by the courts to alleviate conditions of overcrowding and
neglect.

According to a survey performed in New York State, one-third
of the mentally retarded persons living in these institutions could have
remained in the community if alternative local services had been
available (Rosenberg 1969). Large and isolated custodial institutions
for the mentally retarded were initially created to remove them from
the complexities of the modern, urbanized, and industrialized environment (Wolfensberger 1969, pp. 94-100). The ideal of creating asylums
for those who could not compete led to the development of these protective residences, emphasizing "benevolent shelter" (Wolfensberger
1969, p. 97). Ironically, the courts have now ruled that these facilities
provide little protection and may be hazardous to the well-being of
their inmates.

State agencies have attempted to create alternative living arrangements to large and isolated institutions. Rather than build additional residential units and hire more staff at these large campuses,
some mental health agencies have attempted to return state school
patients to the community, either through independent living arrangements, or through foster care or community residential facilities of
various types. In the past, the only patients who ever returned to community living were, for the most part, those who ran away from state
schools and successfully adapted to life outside, or a highly selected
population of borderline normal persons who were for the most part
inappropriately placed in custodial care in the first place (see Edgerton 1967). Now large numbers of mentally retarded persons are being
resettled, some with few adaptive skills for independent community
living.

There are few studies of the utilization of community-based
services for the retarded adult because the efforts to create effective
halfway houses, hostels, and group homes are very recent. Consequently, policy formation in the area of relocation suffers from a lack
of information on what kind of community-based facilities improve
the quality of life and facilitate adaptation for mentally retarded persons. The movement to deinstitutionalize and relocate the mentally
retarded in their home communities has not been approved by all professionals and parents. Relocation often is a priority which clashes
with other desired ends, such as improving physical conditions and
programs at state schools. One specialist in mental retardation services has observed that

Opponents of the view to totally abolish institutions
point to the experience in many states of moving

individuals into group homes, with consequent worse care
and far less supportive services than the large institutions
provide. In some states, increased placement in the community is accompanied by markedly reduced admissions
and thus rapid overloading of the service delivery system.
The diversion of state and federal funds from the institution to the community tends to further deterioriate the
quality of care in these facilities and exacerbate the very
conditions in urgent need of remediation. (Begab 1974,
p. 27).

The question of what happens to mentally retarded adults who
are relocated from state schools constitutes an area of major interest
to practitioners and funding agencies. Research, according to Begab
(1974, p. 18), should be given the highest priority if improvements are
to be made in the care and treatment of the mentally retarded in American society.

The purpose of this book is to examine what happened to
a total of 63 men and women who left three large and isolated state
schools for the mentally retarded and went to live at the community
residence we shall call Gatewood. While an original cohort of 63 persons was resettled, 48 residents who stayed at Gatewood were interviewed three times: first, during their initial week of living at Gatewood to obtain a picture of past activities at state schools; second,
seven to ten months later, to determine the extent to which their lives
had changed; and third, seven to ten months later, to gain further data
on their lives. Among the fifteen who left, four residents had gone to
live with their families, one person moved into the community, and
one had voluntarily returned to a state school; nine were transferred
back to the original state school because of behavior unacceptable to
the staff. One person was struck by a car and killed.

The Gatewood residents were selected from three large and isolated institutions serving a metropolitan area. Screening took place at
the state schools and persons were removed from consideration who
had a history of violent behavior, who required medical care beyond
oral medication, and who were regarded as not capable of either competitive employment, achieving sheltered workshop status, or attending a day center program in the community. Each candidate then
visited Gatewood and was asked whether he would like to transfer.
In a few cases, even when guardians refused to approve the move,
residents who desired relocation were resettled at Gatewood.

The three state institutions from which residents were selected
were among the largest in the United States. One institution was organized on the ward system, while the other two had patients living in
cottage units. Overcrowding prevailed at all three state schools, with

one facility providing 47.5 square feet of sleeping space for each patient when state law mandated 80 square feet. In one of the state
schools, residents lived with 5,000 other patients in facilities designed
for 3,000. The dormitories generally held up to 70 patients and had
available one toilet for every ten residents and one showerhead for
every 40 residents. The three institutions were located in areas far
from the patients' families, with poor public transportation and few
opportunities for working in either competitive or sheltered settings
in the community.

While data were not available about the characteristics of the
populations of the three state schools that provided residents for Gatewood, one state school with which the local developmental disabilities
service was working closely provided some interesting comparisons.
The Gatewood residents were among the least intellectually and func-
tionally impaired of the residents of that school who came from the
geographic area where Gatewood is located. While 87 percent of that
population is considered severely and profoundly retarded, only 16
percent of Gatewood residents are in this category. Gatewood residents were older than the state school population, with only 14 percent
being under 21 as compared to 59 percent in the state schools.

Gatewood compares very favorably to the state schools in fur-
nishings and accommodations. Each resident shares a bedroom with
one other person; every two bedrooms are connected through a shared
bathroom. All rooms in the building are carpeted and well-furnished.
A large lounge area and dining room serve as the major public rooms.
Completed in 1973, the building has a capacity of 70, with a motel-like
appearance both inside and outside. Gatewood was originally designed
as an old age home, but was never used for that purpose. The facility
received the first residents from state schools in March 1973 and
reached its capacity in July of that year. A few residents at Gatewood
came from their family home in the community to fill the remaining
places. Gatewood is owned and operated by a private entrepreneur
who is licensed and regulated by various state agencies. As a community residence, what Gatewood provides on the premises is primarily food and shelter. The staff, however, is responsible for going
outside to secure and coordinate the vocational rehabilitation and
other services required by the residents if they are to make a successful adaptation to community living.

Gatewood is located in an ethnically heterogeneous working
class neighborhood in a large city. The neighborhood consists of
small, attached single- and two-family houses and a large high rise
municipal housing project for low income tenants. The residence is
located near public transportation, stores, recreational facilities, and
churches. There are few factories or large commercial enterprises
in the neighborhood. All vocational rehabilitation services and out-
patient clinic services have to be reached by public transportation.

The people who went to live at Gatewood were mostly adults, with a mean age of 33 years. (This and the following data are summarized in Table 0.1.) There were twice as many men as women; many have lived in state schools for most of their adolescent and adult lives. The mean age at the time of admission to the state schools was 15.7 years and the mean number of years in residence there was 17.7. Before placement in state schools, half of the population was in classes for educable children. When last tested during the past two or three years, the mean I.Q. was 50.8. All persons selected for Gatewood were able to walk, bathe, toilet, dress, and feed themselves. One-third of the population had some medical condition and 16 percent were subject to seizures and were receiving anti-seizure medication when transferred to the community residence. People of many ethnic backgrounds came to live at Gatewood. By virtue of the ethnic composition of the region at the time the population was admitted to the state schools, the predominant groups were Jewish (27%), Hispanic (26%), black (20%) and other whites (27%).

Background of Gatewood Residents

	Male	Female	Total or Mean
White	8	6	14
Jewish	13	1	14
Hispanic	8	5	13
Black	4	6	10
Total Ethnicity	33	18	51
Mean Age	33.1	34.0	33.4
Mean I.Q.	51.4	49.7	50.8
Mean Age at Admission	15.3	18.0	15.7
Mean Years in Institution	18.7	17.3	17.7
Number with Associated Medical Problems	7	7	14

Source: Data compiled by the authors.

We have described the background of Gatewood's organization and the overall objectives of this study, as well as the physical circumstances and social composition of the Gatewood population. In the next chapter we will review the literature relevant to the research problem and describe the methods by which the data for this study were gathered.

REFERENCES

Begab, M. J.
    1974   "The Mentally Retarded and Society: Some Unanswered
            Questions." A paper presented to the Conference on The
            Mentally Retarded in Society: A Social Science Perspec-
            tive. National Institute for Child Health and Human De-
            velopment, Niles, Michigan. April 18-20.
Blatt, Burton
    1970   Exit From Pandemonium. Boston: Allyn and Bacon.
Edgerton, R. B.
    1967   The Cloak of Competence. Berkeley and Los Angeles:
            University of California Press.
Goodman, Walter
    1974   "The Constitution vs. the Snakepit: How Lawyers are
            Proving that Mental Inmates have a Right to Treatment."
            New York Times Magazine (March 17): 21-34.
Rivera, Geraldo
    1972   Willowbrook. New York: Random House.
Rosenberg, A. D.
    1969   Appropriateness of the Continued Institutionalization of
            the State School Population of New York State. Buffalo:
            New York Department of Mental Hygiene.
Wolfensberger, Wolf
    1969   "The Origin and Nature of our Institutional Models,"
            in Robert B. Kugel and Wolf Wolfensberger, eds.,
            Changing Patterns of Residential Services For the Men-
            tally Retarded. Washington, D.C.: Department of Health,
            Education, and Welfare

Resettling
Retarded Adults in a
Managed Community

1

THE PROBLEM OF
RESIDENTIAL CARE
FOR MENTALLY
RETARDED ADULTS

The sociological study of residential care has recently been used as part of an effort to redesign many forms of human services for those who cannot fully take care of themselves. The research efforts on environmental aspects of residential care have focused on the impact of social isolation, under-stimulation, and size of institution on developmental opportunities for mentally retarded persons. Most interestingly, some students of residential care have found that opportunities for stimulation are related more to the operating practices of these organizations than to abstract aspects of institutions such as size and isolation.

INSTITUTIONAL CARE AND BEHAVIOR

There is some evidence to suggest that institutional care induces a "trained incapacity" on the part of patients which might make them maladaptive to community living or even make the staff of state schools reluctant to plan for their return to the community. In a study of the impact of four years of institutional care on children and adults at a state school, for example, a significant decrease in the measured I.Q. of mentally retarded children occurred but the change in test scores for adolescents and adults was not as great (Sternlict and Siegal 1968). Most interestingly, the changes in verbal intelligence were far greater than the changes in performance, ability, or visual-motor coordination. Perhaps the social situation of the state school patient was undemanding in the area of verbal skills. Dentler and Mackler (1961), in a field study of the socialization of retarded children to cottage living, showed that patients were successfully trained by staff for institutional living through the use of rewards and punishments.

Other studies have indicated great variability in residential care
for children. King, Raynes, and Tizard (1971) found important differences in child management practices in residential institutions for
handicapped children. However, no attempt was made in this study to
examine the effects of the practices on the child's self-regard, social
skills, and adaptive behavior.

Contact with staff, at least among mentally retarded children,
seems to have a substantial impact on behavior. M. M. Klaber (1968,
p. 175) found that some of the stereotyped behavior of lower-functioning state school patients would increase and decrease during the day
according to anticipated changes of work shift among the attendants.
It is not clear whether the increase in rocking described which occurred just before the appearance of the second attendant was the result
of reduced activity just prior to the change in shift or of increased
anxiety about the anticipated change in personnel. This variability
does indicate both the importance of staff activity in influencing patients and the alterability of the patients' behavior.

Interaction among patients at state schools seems to influence
behavior in a way that is not conducive to maintaining stable social
relationships. A study of interaction on a ward for mentally retarded
adults found few mutual friendships and little reciprocity among socio-
metric choices (Miles 1965). The most desired friends were those
very likely to be released and given the opportunity to return to community living; in turn, those who might leave may not wish to establish any personal relationships (Miles 1965, p. 175).

There is some evidence to suggest that mentally retarded residents at state schools are able to manipulate staff to obtain the things
they desire. Dorothea and Benjamin Braginsky (1971), in an experimental study of attitudes, concluded that a highly-selected sample of
mentally retarded state school patients was potentially capable of
acting in ways which would enhance their well-being and promote improvements in their lives. It should be pointed out that this study was
mainly concerned with predispositions to act, as elicited through attitude tests, rather than based on actual observations of face-to-face
interaction with members of the staff.

One of the variables often considered to be important in explaining why residential institutions for the mentally retarded are under-
stimulating and impersonal is the size of the facility. Since American
institutions are generally quite large, it is difficult to specify the
effect of size on behavior of residents and staff. Jack Tizard (1970,
p. 301) points out that over 67 percent of the state institutions for the
retarded listed in the 1962 Directory of the American Association on
Mental Deficiency have more than 500 beds. However, he goes on to
say that it is too soon to generalize that the big institution is a bad
institution (Tizard 1970, pp. 308-9). In his previous work on residen-

tial care for children in England, there was no correlation between size of institutions, size of child care units, staff-child ratios, and type of care (Tizard 1970, pp. 308-9).

Large size creates conditions for the formation of primary groups among attendants which may subvert rehabilitation goals. The social organization of the residence is often considered central to understanding child care practices. Tizard (1970, pp. 308-9) found that when the person in charge of the unit spent a great deal of time in direct contact with the children and delegated administrative and domestic responsibilities, then child-oriented rather than institution-oriented practices prevailed. Supervisors who spent time in direct contact with residents functioned as models for attendants as they provided direct supervision.

M. M. Klaber (n.d., pp. 55-57) found in his study of institutions for the mentally retarded in the state of Connecticut that staff-child ratios were not so important in influencing institutional effectiveness (that is, self-care, intellectual growth, lack of stereotyping behavior) as the overall absolute size of each unit: One attendant with ten children will be more involved with them than ten attendants with 100 children (Klaber n.d., p. 57).

Ongoing social interaction between staff and children varied a great deal, depending on the orientation of the directors of the residential care facility. Where institution-oriented management practices prevailed, the staff "spoke to them much less often, played with them less, and physically handled them much less frequently than did their counterparts in the hostels" (Tizard 1970, p. 309). Klaber (1969, pp. 145-48) also concluded that attendant behavior in state schools was a result of administrative practices, particularly direct supervision. Moreover, psychological and educational factors such as attendants' attitudes and in-service training were not related to institutional effectiveness (Klaber n.d., p. 55).

Other students of institutional life have pointed out how important the role of employees and staff is to an understanding of the social situation of the mentally retarded in state schools (Cleland and Dingman 1970, p. 139). The professional staff members who make policy are rarely in day-to-day contact with the residents of state schools, or with the front-line staff of attendants, aides, and employees who provide the direct care for the mentally retarded in these settings (Morris 1969, p. 255). It seems that it can be far more rewarding for administrators to concentrate on decisions which are related to providing the resources necessary for operating these institutions, and to give up their supervision over direct relations between attendants and patients. The result is that each segment of the staff operates autonomously in encapsulated areas in which each gains control over its social environment in exchange for giving up claims to control in the others' territory.

Mentally retarded adults have been largely ignored in the sociology of residential institutions, except in the ethnographic work of Robert Edgerton and his associates at Pacific State School. Here, the focus has been primarily on the "underlife" of the massive, isolated and impersonal institution (Goffman 1961, pp. 173-320), showing what activities mentally retarded adults are capable of, without the involvement of the staff. In adapting to institutional life, mentally retarded adults have been able to "flesh out their lives" through such conventional practices as "dating" (Edgerton and Dingman 1964), "free enterprise" (Edgerton et al. 1961, pp. 35-41), and engaging in a kind of adolescent opposition to authority (Edgerton 1963). These studies do not indicate which skills acquired by mentally retarded adults are adaptive to life outside the institution and which are not. Indeed, few state schools prepare mentally retarded residents for the transition to community living.

THE TRANSITION TO COMMUNITY LIVING

In his study, The Cloak of Competence (1967), Edgerton provides an interesting account of the adaptation of a small number of mentally retarded adults to community living. Without the benefit (or restrictions) of a community residence, his subjects managed to live independently with the informally-arranged help of a person who became a benefactor for the former state school patient. In this study (1967, p. 12), the sample population's mean I.Q. was 65, hardly representative of the patient population of Pacific State School or any other massive institution for the mentally retarded.

Current efforts in California to return mentally retarded adults to community living have involved extensive use of board-and-care facilities similar to Gatewood. These residential programs are run to make a profit and house 30 or 40 persons, or even more. Lacking supportive services and individualized goals to increase the independence of the residents, the board-and-care facilities are located in the community but do not utilize it for programs in vocational rehabilitation or recreation. Nor do they instruct residents in how to use the community transportation system.

Edgerton has observed that the economic arrangements which reimburse proprietors in these facilities provide few incentives to train residents for independent living. Caretakers operate at a profit when their beds are filled up to the capacity of the program. Consequently there is great reluctance to permit a resident to strike out on

his own unless a replacement is immediately available (Edgerton 1974).
However, other investigators in California have called into question
this judgment about board-and-care facilities. A. T. Bjannes and E.W.
Butler (1974) compared the activities of residents at board-and-care
facilities and other types, including group homes and family care, and
found that the former had more independent behavior. Furthermore,
board-and-care facilities seem to more closely realize the goals of
developing social skills and providing a varied round of life than other
types of residential facilities in the community. Extensive exposure
to the community was found to be an important aspect of reintegrating
former state school patients.

The most dramatic changes in behavior of mentally retarded
persons were made in a small experimental unit, Brooklands, a residential program for children who had previously been in a large institution (Tizard 1964). Organized in such a way that the daily routines
of life were guided by concerns for maintaining a normal home life,
the children at Brooklands were observed to be ". . . able to play socially and constructively, at a level approaching that of their mental
age " (Tizard 1964, pp. 133-34). Before coming to this small experimental unit the children were not able to behave outside of "the nar-
row limits of ward routines" (Tizard 1964, p. 79). The children in
this small experimental unit were also shown to make gains in verbal
abilities and to lose many of the behaviors traditionally associated
with mental retardation (for example, rocking). A matched control
group of children who remained in the traditional hospital continued to
exhibit these behaviors and made few gains in verbal abilities.

In a similar comparison of severely retarded children living in
a small locally-based residential care unit and in a hospital unit,
Kushlick reported change in 9 out of 13 behavior areas (1974, p. 10).
Statistically significant changes between the scores of the two groups
at two points in time were reported in the areas of eating, dressing,
and appropriate general behavior. Children who were nonambulatory
made the most progress in the comparison between those who lived
in locally-based units and their counterparts who remained in hospital
care (1974, p. 12).

While these two experiments in England showed that children do
make important gains in behavior, there are no comparable studies on
the mentally retarded adults who make the transition from one social
environment to another. There is a general lack of longitudinal comparisons which can substantiate the claims made about the advantages
of community living for mentally retarded adults. Possibly the intellectual deficits of mentally retarded adults are so great that life for
them is not affected by different social environments. Along the same
lines, severely limited adults may not be able to acquire the social
skills necessary for satisfactory adaptation to urban life.

RESEARCH PROBLEMS AND METHODS

It is reasonable to expect that the social environment of a state school structures the behavior, attitudes, and social relationships of the mentally retarded persons living there. Consequently, when such persons move to another social and physical environment, changes in behavior, attitudes, and social relationships may be expected. Specific questions remain concerning how much change will occur, in what areas of living will change be most dramatic and significant, and whether changes in social expectations for mentally retarded adults are accompanied by new attitudes towards one's self. What kinds of new experiences does community living in a residence provide, and what is the meaning of these new experiences? Are new aspirations acquired which are suitable and appropriate for their new social status as members of the community and appropriate for their level of functioning? Are relationships with family and friends subject to alteration and in what direction? To what extent does decision-making pass into the hands of these newly-resettled mentally retarded adults and with what consequences? How much independent and self-determined activity takes place both at the residence and in the larger community? To what extent to residents participate in the wider community?

These practical questions which can be answered through research may provide some help to policy makers concerned with the consequences of their decision to resettle mentally retarded adults in the community. Curiously, the resettlement of former state school patients in the community has not created the same public controversy that has accompanied similar efforts with former state psychiatric patients (Schumach 1974). Perhaps there are some lessons to be learned from the experiences of the mentally retarded and those mandated to care for them which can be applied to the situation of the former state psychiatric patient.

The meaning of social institutions and their impact on the way we live and particularly on those who are considered incapable of caring for themselves may be illuminated by the findings reported here. Special-purpose organizations have often been given complete control over the fate of large numbers of persons deemed incapable of caring for themselves and/or thought to be a danger to themselves and others. Central to such "caretaker" organizations are three tasks: (1) the need to maintain internal order and coordination; (2) continued reaffirmation of the rightness of the initial judgments made about persons designated as convicts, mental patients, and residents (some of the more popular labels applied to inmates); and (3) safeguarding the public from the inmates. Sometimes it may be conceived that such organizations, through their practices, confirm the need for their existence by calling forth in their wards evidence of "personal maladjustment" and "social incompetency." Alternatively, sheer neglect and understimulation may produce behaviors which are regarded as bizarre and inappropriate but may, in actuality, be the only possible way for inmates to express their unfulfilled needs. Organizationally, these behaviors operate in a self-serving and self-fulfilling way to justify the need for tight control over the inmates' lives.

Erving Goffman's brilliant essays on how the self is structured in "total institutions" suggest that much that passes for a person's typical aberrant behavior is situationally and institutionally induced (Goffman 1961). Regrettably, both for inmates and for the student of human behavior, there are few opportunities to observe persons in very diverse, institutional settings, where the elements of social structure will perhaps vary in influencing patterns of conduct.

One way to support or refute Goffman's assertions about self and social situation is to assess the impact of modification of the environment on people who have lived in total institutions. Few students of populations living in total institutions have been able to observe people before or after having lived in such an environment. Only by having the same population live under different, contrasting conditions can it be determined whether and how much of the behavior of persons in total institutions results from living in such places. A new social environment may enable former inhabitants of total institutions to present themselves in a distinctly different way than in their former place of residence, perhaps producing fewer instances of their former, typically aberrant behavior.

The movement of mentally retarded adults to the community from the large and isolated state school may be considered a natural social experiment about the impact of environmental social change on adaptive behavior and social skills. In a larger sense, the fate of these intellectually limited men and women represents the more complex social reconstruction involved in creating new institutions to meet unfulfilled human needs. If the mentally retarded can undergo personal change in adult life, then why can't other segments of our society be considered as capable of increased realization of their potential?

The findings reported here can shed some light on practical concerns of social policy and on theoretical issues. Through participant observation and standardized open-ended interviews (see Appendixes A and B) conducted at three points in time—during the resident's first week at Gatewood, some seven to ten months later, and again, seven to ten months after the second interview—data were collected on the experiences of the persons resettled. During the first six months of the project a major effort was made to conduct field observations in order to verify and supplement interview responses.

Participant observation—65 hours in all—began at the state school and continued at Gatewood. Upon these occasions informants voluntarily provided important anecdotal information about their experiences at Gatewood. Members of the staff were particularly helpful in expressing their concerns and problems in making policy for this new facility.

The interviews were generally conducted in privacy and were concerned with self-image, interpersonal relationships, work experience, use of leisure time, personal decision-making, and social competency. One person refused to complete an initial interview and was not reinterviewed. Comparisons have been made between answers received during the first, second, and third interviews, to assess whether change has taken place, and in what direction.

This report is organized according to both the temporal and spatial logic of resettlement: first, the initial description of life in state schools will provide a sense of how former patients saw themselves and others; then, we shift to an analysis of the origins of Gatewood and its social organization; next, returning to the interview responses, we examine the positive and negative reactions to resettlement, the extent of change and constancy in aspirations of residents, the availability of new social experiences, the extent to which relationships with family and friends were modified, and the extent to which there were changes in personal decision-making and independence in daily life, including social competency; and finally, we examine the respondents' participation in the wider community.

Any report of experiments or new programs for the mentally retarded in society must carry with it a caveat, namely, that reforms in this field must be treated with a healthy skepticism. Patients are now considered residents, but the mentally retarded have been subjected to manipulation before and have often been bitterly disappointed. We can best begin this report with the comments of one of our respondents, an articulate and cynical observer of foibles and fads in the field of mental retardation, who had observed new programs before in her career in residential care:

> When I first went there—you're going to laugh—they used to call them inmates. . . . And inmates is in those places for wayward souls, you know, like Sing Sing, Alcatraz and all those places. And who ever heard of an institution patient called inmates? And from inmates they went to patients and from patients now to residents. What'll it be next? And here so far it's just people.

REFERENCES

Bjannes, A. T. and E. W. Butler
　1974　"Environmental Variation in Community Care Facilities
　　　　for Mentally Retarded Persons." American Journal of
　　　　Mental Deficiency 78: 429-39.

Braginsky, Dorothea D. and Benjamin M.
　1971　Hansels and Gretels: Studies of Children in Institutions
　　　　for the Mentally Retarded. New York: Holt, Rinehart,
　　　　and Winston.

Cleland, C. C. and H. F. Dingman
　1970　"Dimensions of Institutional Life: Social Organization,
　　　　Possessions, Time and Space," in Alfred A. Baumeister
　　　　and Earl Butterfield, eds., Residential Facilities for the
　　　　Mentally Retarded. Chicago: Aldine, pp. 138-61.

Dentler, R. A. and B. Mackler
　1961　"The Socialization of Retarded Children in an Institu-
　　　　tion." Journal of Health and Human Behavior 2: 243-52.

Edgerton, R. B.
　1963　"A Patient Elite: Ethnography in a Hospital for the Men-
　　　　tally Retarded." American Journal of Mental Deficiency
　　　　68: 372-85.
　1967　The Cloak of Competence. Berkeley and Los Angeles:
　　　　University of California Press.
　1974　"Issues Relating to the Quality of Life Among Mentally
　　　　Retarded Persons." A paper presented to Conference
　　　　on The Mentally Retarded in Society: A Social Science
　　　　Perspective. National Institute for Child Health and Hu-
　　　　man Development, Niles, Michigan. April 18-20.

Edgerton, R. B. and H. F. Dingman
　1964　"Good Reasons for Bad Supervision: 'Dating' in a Hospi-
　　　　tal for the Mentally Retarded." The Psychiatric Quar-
　　　　terly Supplement, Part 2, Utica, N.Y.: State Hospital
　　　　Press.

Edgerton, R. B., G. Tarjan, and H. F. Dingman
　1961　"Free Enterprise in a Captive Society." American
　　　　Journal of Mental Deficiency 66: 35-41.

Goffman, Erving
　1961　Asylums: Essays on the Social Situation of Mental Pa-
　　　　tients and Other Inmates. New York: Anchor Books.

King, Roy D., Norma V. Raynes, and Jack Tizard
　1971　Patterns of Residential Care: Sociological Studies in
　　　　Institutions for Handicapped Children. London: Routledge
　　　　and Kegan Paul.

Klaber, M. M.
    1968   "Stereotyped Rocking—A Measure of Institution and Ward
            Adequacy." American Journal on Mental Deficiency 73:
            13-20.
    1969   "The Retarded and Institutions for the Retarded—Pre-
            liminary Research Report," in Seymour B. Sarason and
            Doris John, eds., Psychological Problems of Mental De-
            ficiency. Fourth Edition. New York: Harper and Row.
            pp. 148-85.
    n.d.   Retardates in Residence: A Study of Institutions. West
            Hartford, Conn.: University of Hartford Press.

Kushlick, A.
    1974   "Epidemiology and Evaluation of Services for the Men-
            tally Handicapped." A paper presented to Conference on
            The Mentally Retarded in Society: A Social Science Per-
            spective. National Institute for Child Health and Human
            Development, Niles, Michigan. April 18-20.

Miles, A. E.
    1965   "Some Aspects of Culture Amongst Subnormal Hospital
            Patients." British Journal of Medical Psychology 38:
            171-77.

Morris, Pauline
    1969   Put Away: A Sociological Study of Institutions for the
            Mentally Retarded. New York: Atherton Press.

Schumach, M.
    1974   "Halfway Houses For Former Mental Patients Create
            Serious Problems For City's Residential Communities."
            New York Times, January 21, p. 31.

Sternlict, M. and L. Siegal
    1968   "Institutional Residence and Intellectual Functioning."
            Journal of Mental Deficiency Research 21: 119-27.

Tizard, Jack
    1964   Community Services for the Mentally Handicapped.
            London: Oxford University Press.
    1970   "The Impact of Social Institutions in the Causation, Al-
            leviation and Prevention of Mental Retardation," in
            H. Carl Haywood, ed., Social-Cultural Aspects of Men-
            tal Retardation. Pp. 281-340.

Wolfensberger, Wolf
    1969   "The Origin and Nature of Our Institutional Models," in
            Robert B. Kugel and Wolf Wolfensberger, eds., Changing
            Patterns of Residential Services for the Mentally Re-
            tarded. Washington, D.C.: Department of Health, Edu-
            cation, and Welfare. Pp. 59-172.

2

THE SOCIAL LIFE OF
ADULT STATE SCHOOL
PATIENTS

While state schools have been condemned by outsiders and by proponents of new forms of human services, they have rarely been examined directly from the perspective of the mentally retarded patients who live in them. One way to find out how those persons who live in state schools are affected by their environment is to ask them about their day-to-day activities and then attempt to present a meaningful description of how they live. Whatever intellectual deficits are present among those regarded as mentally retarded, state school patients are aware of the social consequences of living at a state school and, on the other hand, in their argot, "living free."

Ethnographic study of state schools and those released from them utilized as informants mildly mentally retarded adults who were aware of their situation and of the meaning of being a state school patient. Robert B. Edgerton and F. Sabagh (1962) have described the career cycles of disaffiliation and reaffiliation undergone by mentally retarded patients and their consequent changes in self-image. The stigma and mortification of placement in a state school are also evident in the behavior and anxieties of those released into the community. Former state school patients were concerned about whether their neighbors and employers knew about their former status and some sought to conceal it (Edgerton 1967).

This chapter examines the ways in which mentally retarded adults in state schools who are now living at Gatewood (1) identified themselves; (2) identified others; and (3) described and evaluated the social relationships which they entered with fellow patients and staff members of state schools. The impressions presented here are derived mainly from the unsolicited comments made while answering questions during the first interview and also from the distribution of answers to specific questions contained in the interview schedule. In

11

order to understand fully the successes and failures of the respondents
in the urban environment, it is necessary to describe how the social
structure at state schools shapes the experiences available.

Recent observations about the environments of state schools
(see Kugel and Wolfensberger 1969) make it possible to demonstrate
substantial agreement between the former state school patients' perceptions of social life and the social structure of state schools. By
presenting a description of the social structure, we can better understand the day-to-day lives of retarded persons in state institutions and
how this experience influences their reintegration into the community.
This effort is guided by the dictum of C. C. Cleland and H. F. Dingman (1970, p. 139), who comment:

> In any discussion attempting to convey findings of re-
> search on the characteristics of life of retardates, it is
> essential, if such results arise from investigations on
> institutionalized retardates, that the sociocultural milieu
> of the institution be described to provide a perspective
> to the reader. The role of the employees and staff of in-
> stitutions requires attention because in numerous ways,
> formal and informal, these individuals structure the lives
> of the retarded.

The following discussion of the social structure of state schools
for the mentally retarded is a partial attempt to describe this milieu.
This description is based on direct observation and the observations
of others (see, for example, Philips and Dingman 1968). Some impli-
cations for the development of interpersonal skills required for living in a small residential facility in an urban environment are suggested.

SOCIAL STRUCTURE

Social structure may be defined as the conditions which make
for uniform patterns of conduct of persons who are linked to each
other through interdependent roles. Thus, for example, specific modes
of interaction occur between fellow employees at a workplace and between the employees and employers, resulting from similarities and
discrepancies in power to make decisions in work, security of position, social distance, and so on. While social structure in the form
of interdependent roles shapes everyday interactions, there is rarely
a one-to-one correspondence between the two. Many of the roles that
people perform permit them a wide range of contact with others and

may be considered the locus for the formation of voluntary and informal social relationships.

In everyday life, structured opportunities exist for establishing and maintaining informal social relationships, particularly among people who live or work at the same place. These relationships may be characterized by a good deal of personal expression, joking, and deliberate reductions of social distances by license taking or extending rights to others. Informal relationships depend, however, on persons being able to demonstrate that they regard each other as more than just a means to an end. Such occasions may be available or unavailable, depending on the extent to which opportunities exist to step outside of the formal and specific nature of socially assigned roles. Social structure, then, provides the conditions under which social life occurs.

The highly differentiated nature of the division of labor in urban society produces a social life and culture which is larger and richer than that required by formal organizations and other collectivities to accomplish their goals and maintain themselves. This tendency, it is suggested, results from the inevitable curiosity built up about the lives of others when they are not in our presence. The separation of home and workplace produces two separate worlds which people belong to at the same time. Since all members of society develop this curiosity and in turn take into account that others also have it, ways of talking about oneself are developed and people are expected to talk about themselves during the work day or while at home. Much of the conversation between workmates, for example, has to do with life off the job and/or gossip about those who are not present for the moment. Secrecy is a structural aspect of the organization of modern life and the telling of details about life beyond the job or home is a way of developing social relationships.

What happens, however, when social life is a virtual image of the social structure? What happens when there is no institutionally sanctioned distinction between public and private life? If there is no distinction between private and public statuses for residents, would there be any necessity to develop differentiated roles based on these conceptual distinctions?

Persons who regard themselves as "worthwhile to know" need the time and the place to have others demonstrate to them that they are worth knowing and the opportunities to elicit this behavior. In state schools, the social structure severely limits the social occasions in which support can be generated (Phillips and Dingman 1968). Tight coordination and scheduling, particularly for those whose competency is limited, reduce the number of occasions on which personal information can be presented and garnered in social interaction between staff and patients. By virtue of the expectations for performance that they must fulfill, staff members spend much of their time meeting schedules and making sure that forms are filled out, rather than talking with patients and planning individualized activities to meet developmental goals.

Although Edgerton and his collaborators (1961, 1963, 1964) present evidence of informal patient interaction, opportunities for it are limited in most state schools. Along with scheduling, much of the physical environment at state schools is planned to prevent harm to the life and limb of the patients. This leads to limited privacy for patients and very little separation of public and private spheres. Under such conditions, persons cannot engage in private supportive interchanges by inviting someone into their room, and in so doing, revealing how they live, a privilege that most of us on the outside have every day. Similarly, there are few places to establish deviant identifications with others, often a source of self-regard for those who have been denied more legitimate means of social solidarity (Edgerton and Dingman 1964). Most officially sponsored activities in state schools, such as parties and dances, are not generated by the patients; rarely are they created in groupings that resemble the size of social gatherings in everyday life. Identification with small groups is very limited when mass activities take place.

Since safety and avoidance of injury are major goals in state schools, patients do not have an opportunity to engage in efforts in which they can make amends for failing to fulfill their obligations. Patients are simply not given the opportunity to correct mistakes, particularly when tight coordination and scheduling occur. Moreover, one error or incompetence in one aspect of living is used as evidence by the staff to confirm a patient's need to be confined, to be in a locked ward, or to be under continuous supervision, limiting even further the opportunity to establish relationships.

The rules of social identity, that is, definitions of who is to be regarded as a member of a certain category of persons and who is to be permitted to be present on certain social occasions, are set by the staff and not by patients at state schools (Goffman 1963, p. 3). As a result, any sense of self which is based on allegiance to these rules will necessarily be based on patients seeing themselves as dependent and unable to care for themselves. Public life at a state school, as elsewhere, provides occasions for reaffirming the rules of identity, but these rules are not supportive of the self which patients wish to present. This discrepancy between rules and desired identity is evident in the way many patients deny that they belong there and engage in what may be called rituals of avoidance, seeking to keep others at a distance from themselves, particularly lower-functioning patients or those who engage in bizarre behavior (Edgerton 1963). Patients will often become uninterested in their peers, showing little concern for a fight or for another patient who is having seizures or hallucinating, even when the event is occurring right next to them. A lack of concern for surroundings often indicates a need to preserve oneself in an environment which does not support the self desired.

The Gatewood residents were interviewed about their activities at the state schools in order to obtain a picture of their daily round of life. While referred to as patients at state schools, they were used to serving others more than they were provided with services. They fell somewhere between the totally disabled patients who needed maximum care and supervision and the attendants who provided it. Half of the respondents said they had worked while at the state schools, for the most part caring for and feeding less able persons, cleaning the ward where they lived, or doing odd jobs such as helping to pick up papers on the ground or loading or unloading service trucks. Five residents had steady work in one of the many service shops which provided supplies, repaired buildings or clothing, or did other forms of maintenance. One person had helped the shoemaker and another had had a hand in delivering supplies from the storeroom to the ward buildings. Two women worked in the sewing room repairing torn clothing; these were the only people at Gatewood who had received the legal minimum wage for the work they did at the state school. A large portion of the women's pay had gone to the state school, in partial compensation for their support. Income of pay for residents usually meant a tip, for work done for attendants, in the form of money or food, which was often used in lieu of cash.

Three residents worked off the grounds doing day labor at local restaurants, garages, or bowling alleys, or doing domestic service. One man earned the nickname of "the nightbird" from the staff because of his late hour of return from work as a dishwasher in restaurants in the towns near the state school. In no cases were any residents involved in vocational rehabilitation, either at the state school or in nearby communities.

The lack of available public transportation made working in the community difficult. Isolation in the countryside or in low-density residential areas made travel in and out of a state school very time-consuming. Public transportation in these areas was limited to movement to and from the metropolitan area; travel from town to town was dependent on the use of automobiles, taxis, or buses operated by the state school. The "nightbird" recounted how he often had had to walk long distances back from his place of employment to his dormitory because he did not have enough money for a taxi.

Programmed activities at the state school were geared toward adult education or occupational therapy, comprising about ten hours per week, or two hours per day. A quarter of the Gatewood residents listed these programs as the major daily activity. Adult education and

occupational therapy were regarded as not very satisfying and were
discussed with little enthusiasm or interest. Attendance at these programs was compulsory and two residents told interviewers that they
skipped them regularly and were punished by being locked up during
hours when they were not scheduled for a program. In addition, those
who cut classes were escorted by attendants to the programs and back
to their dormitories.

Twenty percent of the respondents said that they did nothing
during the day at state schools or that they sat around the day room,
generally watching television. No one seemed enthusiastic about this
inactivity but they also did not mention any self-initiated activities,
such as playing ball with other residents or having conversations.

For many of the Gatewood residents who had worked regularly
with an employee of the state school, "the job" was an important way
of organizing their lives. Contact between the "boss" and the state
school resident could be warm and affectionate as well as a way of
"keeping busy" or "staying out of trouble." Residents appeared to
welcome any work experience. Some people who did not have steady
work often mentioned that they had once helped to move beds, or had
gone up to distant state schools to pick up some equipment with employees in a trailer truck, indicating that these moments were important in their lives.

Independent entrepreneurial work was also possible as a way of
making money. A few respondents reported that they washed and waxed
cares or shined shoes on the days when employees received their bi-
weekly pay checks. In addition, money could be made by receiving
tips from attendants for going to the institution's community store for
refreshments. Residents were very proud of earning money at the
state schools and complained about others who stole money from
them. The lack of cash was a universal problem for all residents, and
they were enthusiastic about opportunities to perform a service for a
staff member.

Spending as a daily activity was possible but did not take place
very often on the grounds of the state schools. Residents received an
allowance for clothing and incidentals from the Social Security Administration's Aid to the Disabled, which was credited directly to
their accounts at the state school. These funds paid for such items
as special toilet articles and refreshments at the community store,
but residents did not pay in cash or have control over deductions
from these funds. Choice of items was generally limited to a few
standard commodities, and a few residents said that these stores did
not stock the things they wanted to acquire, such as watches, radios,
or fashionable clothing.

Gatewood residents reported that recreation, entertainment, and
opportunities for socializing were generally organized at state schools

as mass activities, such as movies, dances, and parties related to holi-
days. One resident viewed these programs as not providing satisfying
social contact, with the summer recreation program being better for
him than that of other seasons because volunteers from neighboring
communities were present. There were few occasions that presented
the opportunity for informal socializing, particularly cross-sex social
contact. Men and women ate their meals in large, sex-segregated
dining halls, noted for their noise. At any meal one might sit at a
large rectangular table; five hundred residents might be served at one
sitting. Places for quiet conversation or solitude were few and far
between at the state schools, and residents had a difficult time finding
privacy.

Some cross-sex social contact did take place between residents
outside of the sponsored activities provided by the staff. A fleeting
smile exchanged between residents was often suggested by respondents
as the basis for regarding the other as a sweetheart. Residents often
said they were too shy to tell others of their fondness for them or often did it indirectly through teasing. Respondents admitted that their
sweethearts did not always feel the same way towards them. Having
a boyfriend or girlfriend was regarded as a desired status, even when
the love went unrequited.

Sexual activity between residents did take place at the state
schools. What the psychiatric hospital patients humorously refer to
as "bush therapy" seemed to be a common unsponsored activity. Il-
legitimate births among the women at state schools did take place and
new policies permitted the performance of therapeutic abortions on
patients. State school policy did not permit birth control information
or contraceptives to be dispensed.

For most Gatewood residents, contact with the wider community
outside of the state school was limited to either visits by parents or
visits to parents' homes. Parents were more likely to visit residents
than residents were to go to their parents' homes. Only one person
said he was able to travel to his parents' home by himself. Only 25
percent of the residents claimed to have celebrated their birthday
with their family; 25 percent of the residents had no family contact
at all.

The development of interpersonal relations between resident
and attendants was made difficult by the conditions of the staff's work.
Contact with overworked attendants was on the basis of three work
shifts. Because of the low rate of pay, difficult working conditions,
and shift work, there was a turnover rate of fifty attendants per month
out of approximately eighteen hundred at one state school, with few
replacements available due to economies in the state budget. Attendants seemed to know little about the lives of the people in their
wards. A day attendant could not say whether a patient received medication if the medication was given during the evening hours.

INTIMACY AND IMPERSONALITY

Naming is one way to study how people place themselves in the social structure and what they see as their contribution to it and their commitments to others (Strauss 1959). There is much to be learned from the names used by state school patients to designate persons with whom they came into contact during the course of their stay. The names given to actors within the major categories by former state school patients indicate how they think about them; furthermore, it also tells us a lot about their social relationships and their self-image.

Beyond the global classifications—patients and staff—there are ways that patients have for describing others, which indicate specific persons, the powers they have in their lives, and their significance to each particular patient. Personal identity, as defined by Goffman (1963, p. 57) "has to do with the assumption that the individual can be differentiated from all others and that around this means of differentiation a single continuous record of social facts can be attached . . . to which still other biographical facts can be attached." If the way in which patients designated others in their lives at state schools is examined, it is possible to describe the nature of their social relationships and the sense of self created. Patients would refer to staff members by title; for example, shoemaker, driver, social worker; they used general categories, for example, employee, staff, attendants; they talked about the persons who performed the role, for example, the ladies, the man; finally, the period of work or shift was used, for example, the midnight attendant, the morning attendant. Rarely were attendants or other employees referred to by their last name or by any intimate relationship or bond between the person and an employee (for example, "my friend"). One person, an exception, affectionately called the shoemaker, for whom he had worked for many years, "my boss."

While references to members of the staff of state schools were generally impersonal, so were designations of other patients. Respondents called others in the same situation patients or "the kids." Sometimes "kids" was used to designate lower-functioning persons other than the speaker; "vegetables" was also used in this way. The terms "boys" and "girls" were always used to refer to peers. Ethnic modifiers were employed to identify a specific patient, for example "that colored kid." Other specific patients were rarely referred to as friends or some equivalent. "Bigshot" was used to name other patients who either consistently took advantage of others on a ward or who tested out the newcomers at each building.

In the names used to locate staff and patients in their interviews there was an absence of any reference to self or other patients according to jobs performed in the state schools. Although many patients claimed to have worked, full-time jobs were scarce. Similarly, patients did not refer to themselves according to location, that is, building or ward; they did not regard themselves as sharing social space with others or as being part of a social relationship based on location. No terms were utilized to indicate roommates, bunkmates, wardmates, neighbors, and so on. In contrast, these same persons were quite able to use such referents in describing their relationships while living at a community residence.

Some of the black and Puerto Rican former patients used the argot of the black community to identify themselves as brothers, soul brothers and sisters, indicating that they were capable of regarding some relationships as solidary even when living at state schools.

SELF-IMAGE

Former patients often expressed their sense of self in terms which denied their association and identification with those who were less able and those who could not take care of themselves, including the physically disabled or "infirms." A frequent comment was "I'm one of the bright ones" or "I'm not one of those vegetables." Continuous or frequent contact with the profoundly retarded may be regarded by the moderate or mildly retarded patient as a kind of contamination of self. The staff quickly recognize the humiliating features of this contact and may punish a higher-functioning person by locking him up on a closed ward with the profoundly retarded. As one ex-patient said, "They put you on C Ward and treat you like an idiot." Some patients attempted to distinguish themselves from either the person who is idle during the day (referred to by the staff as "the day room sitter"); from the person who either begs money or favors from the staff; and from the person who is generally not accorded any special rights by the staff (one who never gets the opportunity to stay up very late and eat with the night attendants or watch television with them). One former patient said that he was different from other patients because he did not hang around the supervisor's office; another took great pride because "I works for my money," while still another thought of himself as "always busy and never sitting around." Finally, when staff establish a special relationship with patients this does not go unappreciated and a person may remark that they like a particular staff member because they "treat me like them."

Being a "good" patient doesn't always mean that the person has a positive self-image. The farther removed their daily activities were from the traditional image of the idle and utterly dependent state school patient, the more positive a self-image they expressed. Accordingly, those who were not engaged in some work-like activity described themselves in terms of what they were not or did not do: "I'm no trouble at all." Some women patients claimed to never use bad language, throw chairs, fight, or "lay down for the boys." Males sometimes expressed their innocuousness by saying that they "mind their own business and don't bother nobody." All in all, a good deal of the patients' available self-image is derived from a recognition that they are in conformity with the rules imposed by the staff.

SOCIAL RELATIONSHIPS

A social relationship may be conceived of as containing a name, the terms "governing" the relationship, and its stages of development, the latter element being what does occur and is expected to occur during its existence (Goffman 1972, pp. 191-93). What kinds of social relationships occur in which patients at state schools regard themselves as a partner?

The most salient relationship in the lives of the patients at state schools, according to their own reports, is that which exists with attendants. In contrast to prisons where leadership is provided by a prisoner elite (see, for example, Sykes 1958), the underlife of the state school is dominated by the lower-level staff who come into daily contact with the patients. Patient culture in a state school seems much more derivative of the culture of the attendants than the inmate culture in prisons is of the culture of the guards. For many of the retarded adults in state schools, contact with the attendants is desired, because they do not want to be identified as state school patients and acquire the negative connotation that goes along with it. Relations with attendants were rewarding but at the same time involved extreme dependency; they also clearly reversed the expectations in the relationship concerning who was to serve whom. Attendants were regarded as a source of extra reward, earned by running errands for them. More than two-thirds of the former patients ran errands and received some kind of tip, usually food, soda, candy, or cigarettes. Since there were few alternative sources of reward of this kind, including money contributed for incidentals by parents, these opportunities loomed large in the lives of state school inhabitants. Some ex-patients had more elaborate exchange or entrepreneurial relationahips with attendants and received payment in cash for washing cars, for working in the kitchens, or for helping to take care of the profoundly retarded in the back wards (reported also by Edgerton, Tarjan, and Dingman 1961).

Ex-patients perceived attendants both as providing aid and as doing little. Attendants were considered to be a source of help and protection by over 35 percent of those who responded to a standardized questionnaire about what the attendants did for them. At the same time, almost one-third of those who answered the same question said the attendants did nothing for them. When asked what they disliked about the state school from which they came, almost half of the respondents' negative answers had to do with the attendants. Ex-patients claimed that the attendants were mean to them, blamed them unjustly, mistreated them, and gave them little freedom. These remarks are not merely gripes against those who had power; 20 percent of these former patients voluntarily recounted specific incidents in which they or others had been beaten. Respondents were also asked about what would happen if someone did not want to get out of bed in the morning. Well over half of those who answered said that the patient would be punished; often they added that the attendants would throw the person out of bed, hit him, or pour water on him. Very few former patients thought that the attendants were one of the good things about the state school in which they lived.

Some important characteristics of the relationship between attendants and patients are its asymetrical, compartmentalized, and impersonal qualities. Patients may know a great deal about the families of the attendants but attendants only know about what they see of the life of a patient during their shift. An evening attendant may never know if the patient is visited because visiting hours occur during the day; a day attendant may never know what medication a patient received if it is administered before bedtime. Attendants may witness intimate details of a patients' life, such as their bodies, their defects, their triumphs, and their humiliations. Their relationship with the patients may be characterized as one of intimacy without affection. Similarly, from the point of view of the patients, attendants are regarded by half of those interviewed as the person one goes to see when you need help, or a person one knew while at the state school; but attendants were rarely named as someone the former patient misses from the state school or someone they would like to bring along with them to live or work at a community residence.

Despite the extreme dependence on attendants for rewards and for the necessities of life as well, there was little sense of regret expressed by respondents over leaving the state school when they began living at Gatewood. Social life at state schools was a stage in their lives which had little connection with their current situation. While there was little questioning of the decision to place them in state institutions, the patients did not appear to form very strong bonds with attendants. Observations show that attendants also did not seem to express regret over seeing their patients leave. Once at Gatewood, little contact occurred between ex-patients and attendants from state schools.

Starting with this previous experience, patients from state schools became residents at Gatewood, entering a new social and physical environment. These impressions about how some former state school patients saw themselves and others at state schools imply that their ability to live in the community would be limited. Their acquisition and maintenance of informal social relationships had been strictly limited by scheduling, by the physical environment, and by dependency on attendants. If there are few ways available in state schools for demonstrating alignments with others, so too there were few opportunities to acquire and practice social skills in everyday life; to get others to accept a violation of the rules as a slight or an oversight, rather than as a manifestation of one's limitations; or to learn how and when to justify or explain one's action when things go wrong. The meaning of relocation and the aspirations for community living of these mentally retarded men and women are analyzed in the next chapter.

REFERENCES

Cleland, C. C. and H. F. Dingman
    1970   "Dimensions of Institutional Life: Social Organization,
            Possessions, Time and Space," in Alfred A. Baumeister
            and Earl Butterfield, eds., Residential Facilities for the
            Mentally Retarded. Chicago: Aldine, pp. 138-61.
Edgerton, R. B.
    1963   "A Patient Elite: Ethnography in the Hospital for the
            Mentally Retarded." American Journal of Mental De-
            ficiency 68: 372-85.
    1967   The Cloak of Competence: Stigma in the Lives of the
            Mentally Retarded. Berkeley, California: The University
            of California Press.
Edgerton, R. B. and H. F. Dingman
    1964   "Good Reasons for Bad Supervision: 'Dating' in a Hos-
            pital for the Mentally Retarded." The Psychiatric Quar-
            terly Supplement, Part 2. Utica, New York: State
            Hospital Press.
Edgerton, R. B. and F. Sabagh
    1962   "From Mortification to Aggrandizement: Changing Self-
            Concepts in the Mentally Retarded." Psychiatry 25:
            263-72.

Edgerton, R. B., G. Tarjan, and H. F. Dingman
    1961   "Free Enterprise in a Captive Society." American
            Journal of Mental Deficiency 66: 35-41.
Goffman, Erving
    1963   Stigma: Notes on the Management of Spoiled Identity.
            Englewood Cliffs, New Jersey: Prentice-Hall.
    1972   Relations in Public. New York: Basic Books.
Kugel, Robert B. and Wolf Wolfensberger
    1969   Changing Patterns in Residential Services for the Men-
            tally Retarded. Washington, D.C.: Department of Health,
            Education, and Welfare
Phillips, S. V. and H. F. Dingman
    1968   "On the Construction of Persons." Mental Retardation 6:
            20-22.
Strauss, Anselm
    1959   Mirrors and Masks. Glencoe, Illinois: The Free Press.
Sykes, Gresham
    1958   Society of Captives. Princeton, New Jersey: Princeton
            University Press.

THE CONCEPT OF THE MANAGED COMMUNITY

In the last chapter it was shown that the behavior of state school patients had been heavily influenced by the social organization of the large and isolated custodial institution. In total institutions, particularly those designed to take care of people who cannot fully take care of themselves, most activities are guided by a model of the patient who is seen as capable of doing harm to himself and others. Moreover, this model is fit into the organizational arrangements so that patients are seen as "serviceable objects" rather than as people with needs similar to those of other people and with some capacity to make decisions affecting their own lives. Consequently, the self-image of patients and their social relationships were influenced by the application of this model and this organization of social life at state schools. It provided few structured opportunities for them to see themselves as anything but patients.

It can be argued, however, that any residential institution for the mentally retarded would assume the characteristics of a total institution, given the lack of competency of the residents. Alternatively, given the organizational application of the model of the patient found in state schools, much of the behavior considered to be an aspect of the disability is situationally induced; the patients are constrained by the lack of opportunity to act in other ways.

Gatewood was conceived around a conception of the mentally retarded adult different from that commonly held in state schools. It focused on their abilities as well as their disabilities. It is important to show how the social dimensions of Gatewood differ from those of state schools, and to show the intended and unintended consequences of the planning process which shaped this residence.

24

Gatewood was planned as a formal organization, and sociologically may be considered as constituting a stable association "of persons engaged in concerted activities directed to the attainment of specific objectives" (Bittner 1974, p. 69). Gatewood was planned and sponsored by other organizations. As a product of the activity of actors at other organizations, the role behavior of both staff and residents at Gatewood is influenced by the objectives of these other organizations. The major purpose of establishing this residence in the community instead of in an isolated area was to facilitate the deinstitutionalization of mentally retarded persons.

Some features of Gatewood's social organization are quite similar to those found in total institutions, and some are not. The generic statuses of "staff" and "inmate" are found at Gatewood, as is the scheduling of activities by staff for the residents. But, on the other hand, the physical arrangements of Gatewood provide some privacy for residents and are not conducive to the development of block treatment practices such as mass showers, which are often found at state schools. And Gatewood can never become completely separated because of its location in an urban neighborhood and its functional dependence on other organizations for services such as linens and repairs, and, more importantly, for day programs sponsored by other agencies.

Both by design and because of what actually happened at Gatewood, residents and staff had to cope with the organizations that planned it. This circumstance shaped the organization and practices of Gatewood so that it has not become a total institution. In addition, the planning of Gatewood produced a number of unintended social consequences. Gatewood was conceived as a long-range substitute for the large and isolated state school, and its future funding is dependent upon the ability of the staff to convince other organizations that it is realizing its objectives. Primary among these objectives is the goal that mentally retarded adults who live there lead materially better lives and have opportunities to become reintegrated into the community.

However, by the nature of its activities and the interaction between people who define themselves as part of it and are seen by others as members, Gatewood can be referred to as a "little community" (Redfield 1955).* Unlike other little communities, Gatewood is

---

*Redfield identifies the following characteristics of a "little community." It is distinctive, that is, the boundaries of the community are apparent. It is small in size. Being homogeneous, activities and states of mind are much alike for all persons. Redfield also identifies self-sufficiency as one of the characteristics. Although Gatewood is not totally self-sufficient and probably could not be, given the complexities of modern urban life, it is substantially more self-sufficient than the surrounding larger units.

not encapsulated but is part of a larger urban community. At Gatewood there is a stable pattern of direct contacts with many people from the surrounding urban area and with representatives of diverse social agencies. When conceiving of Gatewood as a little community, special attention must be paid to questions concerning the formation of social bonds between actors, their identification as members, and the formation of a shared set of meanings for interpreting what membership in Gatewood means to members and to the larger social environment. The formation of a community at Gatewood is then a cultural as well as a social development.

Because Gatewood is planned as a residential facility for mentally retarded adults, it is closed off to a certain extent from the rest of society and from other communities. Persons eligible for membership must be over the age of eighteen and legally identified as mentally retarded. Gatewood is then not an "intentional" community based on ideological commitment (Zablocki 1971, p. 53), since its members do not control the criteria for membership. Others affiliated with Gatewood as employees, relatives, or friends may be regarded as having courtesy membership, but are not eligible to reside there. Gatewood should be considered a "managed community," where membership is voluntary but the criteria for eligibility are not in the hands of members.

In a managed community, the potential for social solidarity between members is greater than in other domicilary facilities such as hotels, resorts, boarding houses, or even halfway houses for rehabilitation of psychiatric patients who have been hospitalized. First, the length of stay of residents at Gatewood remains indeterminate; residents are not expected to depart after a few days or even a few months. The expectation is that most of the mentally retarded adults living at Gatewood will not become totally independent and able to move out free of supervision, even though self-reliant behavior is expected to increase. A few residents have been relocated into supervised apartment accommodations but are not fully self-supporting, although they earn their livelihood in competitive employment. These cases are the exception and not the rule. Second, while the residence is not totally isolated it constitutes an ecologically distinct region where there is very high frequency of contact between fellow residents and between staff and residents. Accordingly, there is less frequent contact with those persons, such as neighborhood people, who do not have established traditional or legal access rights to the facility. Furthermore, while residents are not bound to remain at Gatewood but can come and go in an unrestricted way and are in close proximity to the surrounding neighborhood, they tend to prefer to interact with each other. In a complementary way, neighborhood people seem to prefer not to interact with Gatewood residents.

Residing in a managed community implies that besides living with others who are similarly situated, one lives under a certain amount of supervision as well. While privacy is available at Gatewood and residents are free to come and go pretty much as they please, there are rules regulating their conduct. Residents are not permitted to put up overnight guests; nor are they permitted simply to move out whenever they desire without demonstrating that they either have the earning capacity to take care of themselves or are moving into some other protected situation. In the language of the state agency which, ultimately, is legally responsible for the lives of these mentally retarded adults, Gatewood is a "medium-care facility," which reaffirms that Gatewood was intentionally created for others. Gatewood is not merely an organization which provides services for people; it is a community in which people who are similarly situated are in frequent contact. They use this structure of social relationships for interpreting their experience and defining who they are in relation to their fellow residents.

In planning Gatewood, certain assumptions were made about the availability and patterning of services at the facility and in the community. The planners were mainly concerned with developing an environment where people who could not fully take care of themselves would receive needed services, both on the premises and outside; where outside services needed by residents would be arranged by the staff; and where the staff not only made certain that services on the premises are received by residents but that services outside are received as well. The assumed network of services could only be coordinated for residents if they were in close contact with staff in the same physical location. The decision to concentrate relocated mentally retarded adults in one residential facility had consequences for the development of social relationships among them.

While the social relationships among residents and between staff and residents are constrained by this overall plan—since there are formal designations of "staff" and "residents" with reciprocal obligations—these relationships can develop in diverse ways. Reciprocal obligations often expand in an unplanned and informal way, structuring behavior, creating shared meanings and social bonds between people in areas of uncertainty where formal criteria are either incomplete or inappropriate. As the cultural product of a number of organizations, Gatewood is also the social product of the people who live or work there and who have shaped its development as a managed community. In order to explain fully the relationship between the formal and informal dimensions of Gatewood, it is necessary to first describe its planning and consequent development.

PLANNING AND DEVELOPMENT OF GATEWOOD

The large and isolated state schools which came under bitter attack in the early 1970s were planned and populated at a time when few adult services for the mentally retarded were available in the community. Consequently, parents were often urged by human service professionals to place their children in custodial care once they passed the legal age at which education ended for the mentally retarded. While a few sheltered workshops were established for mentally retarded adults as early as 1953, it was not until the mid-1960s that funding available from the Vocational Rehabilitation Services Administration of the Department of Health, Education, and Welfare made it possible for sheltered workshops for the mentally retarded to expand in size and proliferate. Additional funds were raised by voluntary agencies and by contributions from localities which had established community mental health boards.

The state agencies in charge of managing state schools for the mentally retarded decided that it was politically wiser and far more humane to reverse the pattern of long-term institutional care by reducing the populations at these overcrowded facilities. Rather than continue to build large and isolated state schools, these agencies became interested in getting local communities and voluntary agencies involved in operating small facilities and using local services for their residents. Part of this change in policy involved the establishment of regional development services which would encourage other public agencies and voluntary associations to create direct services themselves. Each regional developmental disability service would also be responsible for citizens from their region who resided at the state schools, and would eventually relocate them in the region where they once had lived. As part of the overall goal of decentralizing services, the director of the regional disability service directly involved in the establishment of Gatewood was mandated by the state Department of Mental Hygiene to relocate 50 residents from an overcrowded state school within one year from the date when the directive was issued. The number of residents to be relocated was determined by the proportion of residents from that region or catchment area living at the state school and by the number of residents who would have to be relocated to end overcrowding.

The legislative acts of Congress which brought into being Medicare and Medicaid as third party funding for health services also created stable financial support for services to adults who are chronically ill, physically handicapped, or developmentally disabled. Through the Social Security Administration, financial support for maintenance of persons who could not support themselves was made

available, including payments for care received in health-related facilities such as nursing homes as well as for medical treatment and
hospitalization. Consequently, the mentally retarded adult who was
defined as fully disabled, either permanently or temporarily, could
receive subsidized residential care, involving nursing or other health-
related services.

The funds available for aid to the disabled could not be used for
the construction of residential facilities. However, they could be used
to pay for rents or for residential care rendered by providers of these
services. While initially it was expected that states, localities, and/or
voluntary agencies and associations providing services for the mentally retarded would buy or build the necessary residential facilities,
they did not do so because of several economic and political considerations. Federal expenditures for the Indochina war, as was pointed
out by many observers, drastically affected the outflow of funds into
the budgets of the states and localities, preventing the expansion of
social services in those areas in which the states and localities had
to spend their own funds. Similarly, voluntary agencies such as the
regional Associations for Retarded Children could not count on an increased flow of public funds into their existing programs to enable
them to use funds raised from contributions for new programs.

Deinstitutionalization was never a major goal of the voluntary
associations devoted to serving the mentally retarded. Most voluntary
agencies provided programs for mentally retarded persons already
living in the community, and considered the prevention of institutionalization as a major goal. For agencies already operating community-
based programs, the removal of mentally retarded people from state
schools was not a primary consideration because their parent con-
stituency was already oriented to community services. Many of these
agencies were founded and sustained by parents attempting to create
programs for the mentally retarded children who lived with them. It
is reasonable to expect that they focused their energies on developing
community-based programs for their children. Moreover, official
estimates from the President's Panel On Mental Rehabilitation claimed
that 95 percent of the mentally retarded population lived in the community (1962, p. 3).

Parents of mentally retarded people in state schools were more
likely to join the benevolent associations affiliated with state schools
than to work with voluntary agencies devoted to aiding mentally retarded people living with their families.

Finally, some state agencies and voluntary associations met
with considerable resistance when attempting to buy or rent space in
populated areas for the creation of small- or medium-sized residential
facilities. Community-based municipal or state-run rehabilitation programs for drug addicts were similarly resisted by many communities.

Some people who lived near proposed residences for the mentally retarded may have feared that changes in the composition of the population being rehabilitated could take place without being subject to the
approval of local community planning boards or of the community itself. A more realistic but rarely expressed possibility was that local
services would become overloaded by programs of this kind.

Given this array of factors, resettlement plans were slow in being developed. State agencies involved in establishing residential services in the community were extremely sensitive to the political pressure exerted by outraged constituents on legislators, and did not wish
to antagonize the elected officials who held the purse strings. Directors of state agencies did not wish to have legislative committees in-
vestigate their activities. Officials of the state Department of Mental
Hygiene in the state in which Gatewood is located, as well as candidates
for elective office, were already under attack from the news media
and from irate parents for the poor conditions found in the state
schools. Because of this political climate they were reluctant to plan
and run any additional residential programs, their preference being
to let private organizations or local government do the job.

The proprietors of nursing homes, old age homes, and other
health-related facilities were well aware of the rates of reimbursement available from the Social Security Administration for the care
of the fully physically disabled, the aged, and the developmentally disabled. The proprietor of Gatewood was no stranger to contracting for
care for those persons formerly housed in state hospitals and schools,
since he had already established several residential units in the state
for former psychiatric patients. In addition, he had already discussed
the possibility of helping to reduce the patient population at an extremely overcrowded state school by building and operating a residential service near it.

Gatewood was originally designed as a home for the aged. When
the proprietor of Gatewood inquired as to whether the director of the
regional developmental disabilities service would be interested in establishing an adult residence, the building was almost complete. There
were even brochures available, announcing that a new home for senior
citizens would be opening at the site. It was only after negotiations
between the director of the regional developmental disabilities service and the proprietor took place that the plans were formulated for
the use of the building as a residence for mentally retarded adults.

It would appear that the agencies mandated to provide residential services for people in the local community who could not live
independently were to some extent in competition over how the building known as Gatewood would be used. The director of the regional
mental health agency and the director of a psychiatric hospital were
also interested in creating a residential care setting for formerly

hospitalized psychiatric patients. Negotiations were broken off until the state Department of Mental Hygiene decided who had first rights to negotiate with the proprietor.

In addition, the proprietor was extremely anxious to fill the residence as quickly as possible, in order to begin realizing a financial return on his investment and pay off his creditors. But before Gatewood could be opened as a residence, it had to be approved by several municipal and state agencies. Mental retardation, welfare, and health agencies required a staffing and utilization plan and a program suggesting how this plan would be implemented. This procedure was necessary for acquiring licenses, and involved several months of lengthy negotiations. The major issue under discussion had to do with the number of residents whom the facility would be allowed to serve, with the proprietor seeking to maximize the number of bed spaces and the supervisory agency personnel seeking to maximize living space. The proprietor would realize a higher return if there were more beds available to be filled with former state school patients or community placements.

A second and related issue arose concerning the pace at which staff would be hired. In this regard it appeared that the owner wished to keep costs down by limiting the hiring of personnel who would not be fully needed at first, because the rate of resettlement was slow. At one point, the owner threatened to fill Gatewood with welfare families from single-room occupancy hotels if official approval was not forthcoming for his plan and implementation program.

While these maneuvers were taking place, the regional developmental disabilities service was still in the process of planning its own priorities and its own services for the community. Its total staff was less than fifty people, with the recruitment of other staff and the acquisition of space for its own program being major concerns. Nevertheless, the mandate to relocate 50 patients from the overcrowded state school was seriously approached as a goal that the fledgling regional service should achieve. The lack of available domiciliary space and staff meant that the developmental disabilities service would have to find a provider of such a facility. While residential services were contracted for with the proprietor of Gatewood, other resources were allocated, mainly staff time, to accomplish the task of selection and relocation of patients from the overcrowded state school.

The director and chief of services of the regional developmental disabilities service designated a team of mental health workers to be in charge of resettlement. This team was lead by a community service specialist who later was to be appointed as director of all community services for the agency. The commitment of these personnel to resettlement at this time in the agency's growth involved a major

allocation of scarce resources involving at one time as many as twenty
people. To promote the development of the resettlement team, the
chief of services was actively involved in discussions with the team
members about the criteria listed in Chapter One for selection of the
potential residents, as well as in providing weekly reports regarding
the state of the difficult negotiations going on between officials of the
state Department of Mental Hygiene, the director of the regional developmental disabilities service, and the impatient proprietor of Gatewood. Even after screening of potential residents began at the overcrowded state school, the resettlement team received no assurances
that the facility would ever provide residential services for mentally
retarded adults. This was very demoralizing news to people attempting to make a serious effort not to raise false hopes among state
school patients.

The first screening visit made to the overcrowded state school
included a psychiatrist, the team leader (whose prior employment was
as a teacher of mentally retarded children), a social worker, a psychologist, and a sociologist (the senior author of this study). Aside from
the criteria described in the introduction, the team wanted to include
patients who were not potential dangers to themselves and others.
Gatewood was conceived of as a minimum security facility, with no
physical restraints available for use on residents who might be unable
to respond to other means of social control, such as loss of privileges,
counseling on how to cooperate, or simply close supervision by staff.
In contrast, state schools have their own police and can restrain serious offenders in an institutional jail or move patients from open to
locked wards.

The resettlement team and others from the regional developmental disabilities service were involved in other activities besides
screening potential residents. Contracts had to be made with providers of other needed services if the former state school patients
were to make a successful adaptation to community living. The state
Division of Vocational Rehabilitation was contacted and arrangements
were made for a counselor from that service to be directly available
at the regional developmental disability service to process applications for subsidized placement in vocational rehabilitation programs
in the community. In addition, the voluntary agencies who operated
such programs were also contacted and discussions took place as to
the tuition that would be charged to trainees. Some voluntary agencies
objected to having to defray part of the costs for this service because
a profit-making operator was involved in providing residential services. The voluntary organizations regarded proprietary arrangements
in the field of mental retardation with suspicion, particularly since
the high rate of reimbursement for domiciliary care included few rehabilitation services. Since the agencies which had ultimate authority

as to the approval of the use of proprietary residential care for mentally retarded adults were also partially subsidized by the same voluntary organizations, they were somewhat chary about becoming involved in a controversy over the use of public funds to realize financial
returns on investments made by owners of residential facilities.

STAFFING

The owner of Gatewood remained accountable to the regional developmental disabilities service insofar as the programmatic aspects
of the lives of the residents were concerned. The resettlement team
was particularly concerned about providing a stimulating program for
residents in which they would get out and use the community for a variety of activities, including recreation and medical care. According
to the goal formulated by the resettlement team, activity was desired
but should be directed outward so that the community would be used
by residents; the residents should not be restricted from moving
freely in the community, and should not remain idle and inactive, as
they had been at state schools. The resettlement team was concerned
with the problem of relocation and with avoiding the creation of a
"mini-institution." They did not want the new facility to result merely
in less visible "warehousing" of state school patients. The resettlement team provided advice on matters of training or programs as
problems arose. However, it was not responsible for providing or
training the staff at Gatewood; the staff was hired by the owner.

In order to create a managed community in which living patterns
approximate the normal round of life experienced by ordinary people
in the community surrounding Gatewood, the staff had to share this
goal and know how to implement it. The owner of Gatewood was expected to hire people who were familiar with mentally retarded adults.
The first director of Gatewood was a man who held a master's degree in social work and had extensive organizational experience as
a counselor for the state's Division of Vocational Rehabilitation.
Since Gatewood could not be opened without a license, this person
was initially assigned the task of writing up the program for the facility, including staffing commitments and use of space for program
and dormitory functions. For a mental-health-related program, the
licensing requirements were that a social worker, a teacher, vocational counselor and a recreation worker be employed to provide coordination with outside agencies and to give instruction and counseling.

Hotel-type services were to be provided by a housekeeping
couple who were expected to live on the premises. A number of

positions for mental health therapy aides were also written into the proposal, and there was supposed to be a nurse to oversee the administration of prescribed medication. Physicians in the neighboring community were to be used for primary care, and would be reimbursed through Medicaid. Special medical services were provided at the ambulatory clinics of a local municipal hospital.

While the aides had frequent and direct contact with residents, so did the housekeeping staff. The position of housekeeper proved to be highly unstable in the social organization of Gatewood. Recruitment for the housekeeping couple was by internal selection from the other facilities run by the proprietor. The first housekeeping couple was experienced in operating a domiciliary facility for psychiatric patients who were under heavy medication. They had no familiarity with mentally retarded adults and were overtly anxious about the behavior of the people with whom they would be in frequent contact. The director of Gatewood sensed their uncertainty and encouraged them to request a change of assignment from the proprietor.

The second housekeeping couple had previously worked in another proprietary facility for the owner, this one an old-age home. This couple worked at Gatewood during the first months when state school patients were being relocated. The woman stayed largely in the background, while the man was determined to let the mentally retarded adults know he was the stern but loving patriarch. Aside from coming into very frequent conflict with residents, who found him arbitrary and capricious, he also did not get along with the resettlement team, which had frequent and often heated discussions with him about his behavior with residents. Long before he left Gatewood, the director said that he could not work with this houseparent and that it was already agreed on by the owner and himself that the current housekeepers would be transferred and the roles of housekeeping couple would be redesigned and downgraded. While the director was supposedly in charge of program and the housekeeping couple were to provide support services in the form of meals, maintenance, and cleaning, the role of housekeeper could not be confined to those functions as long as the housekeepers lived on the premises and were asked by aides and residents to coordinate evening and weekend activities and settle disputes. After these experiences with the first two housekeeping couples, the support functions were assigned by the director to newly-hired cooks who simply prepared meals, and to porters and other service personnel who cleaned, and performed other janitorial services.

The salaries provided for the staff positions at Gatewood did little to attract highly qualified workers with experience in working with mentally retarded people. The positions of vocational counselors, social workers or therapy aides paid 25 percent less than similar

positions in the state or city civil service system. The director had
a very difficult time finding qualified people, although the people hired
to be aides were friendly and well-meaning men and women who were
at ease with the residents.

The staff who were hired did not initially know how to perform
their jobs because they were not thoroughly familiar with the goals of
the program or the capacities of the residents. They did not know how
to implement the goals, given the expectations that the mentally retarded adults had for the staff. It is possible that any other staff, even
with some experience and training in the field of mental retardation,
would be faced with the same uncertainty because of the open-ended
character of the new program and the sudden shift in the residents'
situation, from state school to community living. Yet some of the staff
were conspicuously unprepared for the population for whom they were
caring. In anticipation of the arrival of the first adult residents, the
recreation worker went out and bought coloring books, producing be-
wilderment among the new arrivals, who did not see themselves as
children. An aide who had some experience in directing a bowling
program for severely retarded adolescents living in the outside community expressed a great deal of concern about how he would work
with an adult population that was only moderately retarded. He was
most concerned with the question of whether he would be able to gain
the cooperation of mentally retarded adults. His general view was that
the prior experience of the residents in institutional living would make
them difficult to supervise in a more permissive setting.

The resettlement team found the general lack of expertise in the
area of mental retardation among the staff at Gatewood to be as dis-
tressing as the autocratic behavior of the second housefather. Regular
joint staff meetings ensued, which the resettlement team hoped would
establish minimal levels of competency for each member of the staff.
The resettlement team also attempted to provide some short-run, on-
the-job training for aides who were particularly inept when it came
to defining themselves in relation to the residents. First, aides had
a tendency to pick out favorites among the residents, making themselves less accessible to other residents who were not socially skilled
or who were less conventional in appearance and demeanor. Second,
aides introduced a modified uniform so they could be identified as
staff, particularly when on outings with residents in the region around
Gatewood. Most aides were women from the surrounding working
class neighborhood, who did not want to be identified as residents by
neighbors when they were seen in the company of mentally retarded
adults. The resettlement team tried to deal with these behaviors on
the part of aides in terms of their social consequences, that is, the
extent to which they would foster the development of social skills by
residents and the residents' acceptance as part of the surrounding
community.

The director was willing to make alterations in staff practices, although he never permitted the rehabilitation team to screen potential staff for their suitability in working in Gatewood. Perhaps because he was concerned about his autonomy as director, the rehabilitation team was not permitted to become involved in the actual day-to-day operation of the residence.

Recruitment, selection, and training of staff were continuing problems for the director. The available salaries did not attract people with training in human services or those who were highly motivated to work with mentally retarded adults. The staff were never provided a formal training program as a way of overcoming their educational deficiencies or their lack of experience. The plan to relocate only a few state school patients at any one time and to spread over six months the process of filling the facility up to its capacity of seventy residents also made it difficult for the director to develop an awareness of the need to train the staff. It was possible to maintain compliance without special training as long as the residents were very few in number and ample staff were on hand. The budget of the cost-conscious proprietor did not permit mass hiring, and staff were put on payroll a few at a time, thus making it difficult to produce a training program prior to contact with staff and residents.

The lack of training for staff may also have resulted from other aspects of resettlement. The plan for Gatewood did not call for a large-scale therapeutic or rehabilitation program at the residence. Consequently, the director made every effort to find outside services for residents. In addition, he became increasingly dissatisfied with the vocational potential of candidates after the screening at two state schools by the rehabilitation team. He then personally conducted screening at an additional state school, an institution as yet untapped for resettlement in that region by the developmental disabilities service in the city. While his screening procedures did not differ substantially from those used by the rehabilitation team, he did locate some able candidates who were likely to be employable in the community. The screening conducted by the director provided a resident who moved quickly into vocational rehabilitation and then competitive employment. This person adapted so well to community living that he now lives in an apartment with a roommate. Unfortunately, the director's selection process at this alternative state school also brought two young men to Gatewood who were later thought to be responsible for a great many thefts from other residents. Later, these two residents were caught by the police burglarizing a nearby candy store and were returned to the state school from which they came. In general, as will be shown in the next chapter, the higher-functioning residents had more difficulties with staff at Gatewood and also more frequently got into fights with other residents.

While it is interesting to report the director's independent screening effort in terms of its unintended negative consequences, this anecdote was not meant to demonstrate the ineptitude of the director. There is a more significant point here, having to do with the development of the relationship between the Gatewood director and the regional developmental disabilities service. The acquisition of the right by the director to recruit residents from state schools indicates that Gatewood had become a more independent organization. However, it is still dependent upon supervisory agencies for its license and for its rate of reimbursement from the Social Security Administration.

Once established as an operating facility, Gatewood was no longer a sponsored organization solely dependent on the regional developmental disabilities service for continuous approval. The director of Gatewood is now able to spend less time on bureaucratic matters concerning compliance with licensing requirements and program proposals, and to devote more time and energy to dealing with the problems of residents in the larger urban environment and within the managed community. Indicative of this newly acquired independence from sponsoring agencies was the proprietor's eventual hiring of the director to write other program proposals and his replacement by the assistant director whose concerns have been exclusively with running the residence.

The shift in attention away from matters concerning compliance with the directive of state agencies also indicates that Gatewood has achieved some stability as a managed community, reaching a point where internal relations among members and contacts with outside agencies and the larger urban environment have become crystalized. In the next chapter, the social organization of Gatewood will be analyzed, with regard to its functioning as a managed community.

REFERENCES

Bittner, Egon
1974 "The Concept of Organization," in Roy Turner, ed., Ethnomethodology. Baltimore: Penguin Books. Pp. 69-82.
President's Panel on Mental Retardation
1962 National Action to Combat Mental Retardation. Washington, D.C.: United States Government Printing Office.
Redfield, Robert
1955 The Little Community. Chicago: University of Chicago Press.
Zablocki, Benjamin
1971 The Joyful Community. Baltimore: Penguin Books.

In spite of some conspicuous efforts to avoid replication of state schools, Gatewood manifests some of the characteristics of a total institution (Goffman 1961, pp. 3-124). It is somewhat cut off from the surrounding social regions by virtue of its architectural differences, its size, and its sponsorship, as well as by the special characteristics of its population. It is an establishment in which activities are scheduled by one set of actors, the staff, who define themselves and are defined by various legal agencies of control in the society as caretakers for others who are regarded as not fully capable of managing their own affairs even though they possess at least some adaptive skills. Consequently the major social roles of "staff" and "inmate" typically found in total institutions exist resulting from the differences in the power of people with these two statuses to determine the schedule and allocate resources. The restriction on the use of these concepts is that in a community residence "inmates" are not fully cut off from alternative sources of reward and alternative significant others who can define them according to other qualities they possess or other activities they perform.

The single most important problem faced by the director of Gatewood, as was suggested in the last chapter, was finding ways to keep the residents active. Given the limited staff available and the limitations of its expertise in matters concerning the organization of a program, the burden of providing activity fell very much on the director. He initially planned that residents would be out during the day in vocational rehabilitation programs or sheltered workshops in the community. When he attempted to implement this strategy through efforts to start the movement of residents into training programs, he was met with the seemingly unalterable and protracted procedures of the state Division of Vocational Rehabilitation. While some openings were available for trainees at programs in the community, a complete psychological evaluation was necessary before subsidization for 33 weeks of training would be approved by the Division of Vocational Rehabilitation. The cost of the psychological evaluations would be borne by this same state agency through contracts with consulting psychologists. The state Division of Vocational Rehabilitation did not provide any special consideration for this former state school population, but instead treated them as they would any clients who came to them through some other existing referral network. One exception in procedure should be noted: a vocational rehabilitation counselor was assigned by the regional developmental disabilities agency to work directly with the candidates for training from Gatewood. Once this provision was made, it was still often three or four months after applications for support were made before residents were evaluated by consulting psychologists.

No other procedure was implemented to circumvent this delay in placement in vocational rehabilitation settings. The director of Gatewood suggested that perhaps the regional developmental disabilities agency would provide the evaluations, since it had psychologists on its staff. The response to this request was that it was not the policy of the agency to duplicate services already available in the community. The proprietor of Gatewood also did not consider bearing the costs of the evaluations, even though he would need fewer aides during the day if the residents were out attending training programs.

Another possibility was that the voluntary agencies which operated vocational rehabilitation programs could pay for or provide the needed psychological evaluations. In this case, the voluntary agencies operated vocational rehabilitation services partly through subsidization from governmental sources and partly at their own expense. They were, therefore, reluctant to add new expenses by paying for the needed evaluations. Moreover, one voluntary agency involved in training Gatewood residents for competitive employment or sheltered work raised the question about future subsidization. Once the state funds for 33 weeks of training were exhausted, if placement into competitive employment was not possible the trainees would become permanent sheltered workshop employees. It was not clear which agency would bear the cost of monthly tuition at the workshops, since most mentally retarded adults were not able to support themselves in these facilities. The voluntary agencies felt that part of the aid to the disabled payments being made to the proprietor of Gatewood ought to go to pay for the costs of services of staff at their workshops since these reimbursements were supposed to be partly for the provision of rehabilitation and health-related services, not simply for bed and board.

THE USE OF STAFF

The organization of Gatewood was initially based on the nursing home model. First, the concept of supervising areas rather than providing activities was rigorously adhered to in the allocation of the work force. There was a tendency to schedule the same number of aides for each day or shift regardless of whether there was variation in the residents' needs for attention. One aide commented that working on a weekend was very easy because there were few residents around. Secondly, this model influenced the expectations that aides had for themselves, as they tended to see their work primarily in terms of coverage of hours rather than as specific activities performed. There was an initial tendency on the part of the aides to be passive supervisors of health and safety, as they would be in state schools, rather than active instructors in such needed areas as personal hygiene and grooming. Thirdly, there generally was little concern on the part of the aides as to how their behavior might be interpreted by residents or how it might affect the adjustment of residents to community living. While aides, for example, took meals with the residents in the dining room, they were often seen eating either together or with the same two or three preferred residents.

The use of the nursing home concept was particularly inappropriate for mentally retarded adults who were physically able to do many things for themselves and whose major desires were based on the wish to work and earn money. The nursing home concept was evident when, in the first six months before vocational rehabilitation programs, staff members did not devise an alternative program which would get the residents acclimated to living in a city. While the director and his staff were concerned with the lack of vocational activity, they tended to ignore the substantive problem that the residents had lived in state schools for most of their lives and required training to orient themselves to their new living situation.

During this initial period before workshop placements were made available, a number of recreational activities were introduced, and support activities were upgraded in the attempt to deal with the problem of idleness. First, the period of inactivity led the residents to define meals on a fixed schedule as a major activity of the day, much as happens with the elderly and infirm in nursing homes or with patients in state schools. Residents would line up in anticipation of meals long before it was necessary to appear in the dining area. Residents wanted to keep busy and competed with each other for the opportunity to perform kitchen services either in the course of food preparation or in cleaning up. In general, the same people were used in this capacity, as scarce jobs were not rotated to give others the chance to learn new skills or to get a chance to keep busy. Secondly, cleaning of bedrooms and common rooms as well as yard work became major sources of activity for residents. The staff became very concerned about these matters and would remind residents that these were very important activities not to be neglected. During this period the residents spent much of their morning engaged in such tasks as vacuuming rugs, making beds, polishing furniture, and cleaning bathroom fixtures.

Staff did not initially teach residents how to find their own recreation in the community, although later they encouraged this behavior. The model of the immobile nursing home patient was applied in the form of staff preferences for in-house entertainment, usually in the form of documentary films acquired from the public relations offices of companies such as Bell Telephone or from foreign consulates. Residents did not find these films very interesting and preferred adventure films and other entertainments involving trips to other parts of the city or to well-known locations such as sports stadiums and arenas.

DEFINING DEVIANT BEHAVIOR

During this lengthy period of inactivity, the staff had a number of problems related to defining inappropriate behavior for residents. How could it be prevented and what means of social control could they employ? These questions arise in the formation of any new community, but in a managed community, which was regarded as an innovative reform in care for the mentally retarded, they were a special concern. First, the Gatewood staff did not have the means of coercion available at a state school, such as isolation rooms or other ways of separating out deviants. Second, any use of coercion through corporal punishment was ruled out by the supervisory agencies as well as by the beliefs about treatment held by the director. Third, it was difficult to tell whether some behavior with few disruptive consequences was deviant. Appearing disengaged or babbling to oneself may seem harmless to people who know a particular resident, but it may appear different to outsiders, who impute from these attributes lack of control on the part of the person. Fourth, residents were used to employing the working class argot of the street, with the usual complement of obscenities, often employed at inappropriate times and places. Finally, residents were sometimes willing and able to use physical force against others whom they felt were not giving them sufficient respect, by picking up a chair and swinging it, for example.

Much of this behavior was a holdover from institutional life but it still required the development of some boundaries for behavior appropriate for living in a managed community. The director was also concerned about maintaining a staff that was difficult to acquire in the first place; right from the start, any violence against a member of the staff was responded to by immediate transfer back to the state schools. Without such swift punishment staff morale would have been very low and aides would probably have left the job. The director was particularly concerned with maintaining good relations with his work force and was very flexible about permitting the women from the neighborhood who were aides to take extended leaves during the summers so that they could care for their school-age children. The summer months also coincided with the availability of a large number of collage students seeking employment, so that Gatewood had no labor shortage. The evident flexibility in the employment patterns at Gatewood provided no special administrative problems for the director. Moreover, by extending favors to his staff he could call on individuals to work on days when others failed to show up or to stay late under similar circumstances.

Other behaviors of residents, such as appearing withdrawn or disengaged, or having psychotic episodes in public were also considered forms of deviant behavior which required staff attention. Even inappropriate clothing was found irritating by the director, because of his concern for avoiding conflict with neighbors. Residents who stood idly in front of the facility were regarded by the director as a potential source of complaint by neighbors and a few people did register complaints. While Gatewood was regarded as a source of employment by many in the neighborhood, some of those who owned homes nearby were concerned about how the streets were being used for loitering. A nextdoor neighbor suggested that a high fence be erected to prevent residents from staring into his yard. Much of the staring ended after a few months when residents became more accustomed to being among strangers and the neighbor did not make any further complaints.

Interestingly, the use of obscenity became less evident with the passage of time, as residents were removed from contact with employees of state schools who when under pressure used obscenity a great deal to encourage patients to leave certain areas and activities and go elsewhere. Moreover, it was clear that residents did not use obscenity outside of the facility in the streets but only as a means of expression when in conflict with staff or fellow residents. Gradually, residents began to limit their coarse expressions to what were regarded as appropriate times and places.

SOCIAL CONTROL

After six months, staff became concerned about the general problem of access to Gatewood. As an unrestricted facility which rarely had locked doors, Gatewood was open to anyone from outside. Furthermore, no security guard was present to act as a visible deterrent to potential intruders or to question and screen outside visitors. Teenagers from the community had easy access to the common room; they came in and would sit and talk with residents without being asked to leave. The families of residents were not restricted to specific visiting hours, although limits were eventually set on how late outsiders could stay in the evenings. This lack of control over access to the building led to the early disappearance of some office equipment and to the installation of locks on windows and doors leading to these areas.

Initially residents had no locks on their bedroom doors and many personal articles were stolen. Some articles were later recovered in the rooms of other residents but some were never found. After many complaints by residents and some of their families, locks were installed on all bedroom doors and interconnecting bathroom doors. The problem of theft receded substantially although the problem of frequently lost keys has produced a new concern for the director and staff.

Control over outside regions and access to the facility was paralleled by staff concern that residents tended to flood into work areas reserved for the staff. Region control was a major way in which the staff attempted to establish their rights and authority. The kitchen and office were the two major areas in which staff maintained strict control over who had the right to be present. The kitchen staff only permitted the presence only of those residents who were working on food preparation. The office staff regulated the flow of traffic into their area by locking the door to the office and for the most part dealing with residents through a window. Later the window was replaced with a movable opaque shutter, so that staff would not have to attend to importuning residents. Initially, when residents requested spending money from their own accounts they were able to receive it as long as the office staff were present. Later, such requests, as well as requests for carfare to get to workshops, were limited to a few hours in the early evening. Loudspeakers were introduced as a means to announce these events as well as other scheduled activities. In general, bureaucratic rules developed in those aspects of Gatewood's social life where unrestricted contact between staff and residents made it difficult for the staff to carry out its assigned tasks.

While control over scheduling always remained in the hands of the staff, residents had access to the director, who could order changes to suit individual needs as well as make other efforts to resolve complaints. Despite restricted access to certain regions, the major decision-makers who made policy and made individual recommendations and dispositions were available to residents. Residents often anticipated the arrival of the director in the morning and would begin petitioning him even before he could extricate himself from his car. Residents were also admitted to the director's office for discussions of their requests. These occasions also became more formal and more regular when the residents, with the help of the teacher, formed an elected council.

While the council was never involved in establishing rules at Gatewood, it was consulted for advice from time to time about problems that affected the people who lived and worked there. The council, by its selection of a chairman, significantly reflected the aspirations of the residents to be like other people in the community. The chairman, a transfer from another community residence and not in our sample, was a man who had acquired a steady job at a fast-food restaurant, and was socially adept; he owned many consumer items, including his own portable television set. In a sense, his election, as well as ratifying his status as spokesman for others, was part of the process of establishing the ideal rules of identity for residents. Interestingly, the chairman of the council served as a role model in another way, being the first resident to be relocated from Gatewood into a more independent living arrangement, with a family that cared for four other mentally retarded adults.

Once residents became affiliated with workshops, the reduction in time spent at Gatewood had an interesting effect. Fewer incidents were reported which required staff intervention, and internal control was far easier to maintain. In addition, a new punishment was made available to staff. With the cooperation of the staff of the workshop, a resident could be temporarily suspended from his vocational rehabilitation program for deviant behavior at Gatewood. In general, the staff became more tolerant of the "normal" deviant behavior exhibited by residents and tended to regard aberrant behavior as a day-to-day trouble of working with mentally retarded adults. Once outside vocational rehabilitation programs were made a major activity on weekdays, few residents were transferred back to state schools.

In the interest of establishing greater harmony among residents, a number of counseling groups were established at Gatewood, with the participation of psychologists from the regional developmental disabilities service. These group meetings became occasions for criticizing other residents either directly or, more often, indirectly. Complaints were raised about some residents who tried to boss others.

This behavior carried over from state schools where residents had helped to care for severely retarded patients. In addition, the house-keepers at Gatewood had a tendency to call upon one or two residents to encourage the others to retire in the late evening. Some complaints were also voiced about residents who were permitted to stay up as late as they pleased watching television with the aide who worked the 11 P.M. to 7 A.M. shift.

INFORMAL PEER REGULATION

Resident concerns in the area of selective privileges and re-sponsibilities reflected some of the uncertainties and inconsistencies that existed in the formal system of social regulation established be-tween residents. Consequently, some informal group norms developed in response to the problem of how to deal with bossy residents; these objectionable people were subjected to some barbed sarcasm in order to bring them back into line. For the residents these were occasions when the concept of membership in the natural Gatewood community developed considerably. As members of the community one simply did not have to take orders from a peer.

Efforts at informal peer regulation through sarcasm or even ostracism were not always effective in bringing deviant actors into line. A case related to the development of the shared definition of membership and nonmembership presented itself in the way in which staff and residents reacted to one resident, a male who sometimes appeared in women's clothing. While the staff were uncomfortable about his efforts to find homosexual partners both at Gatewood and throughout the city, they were not as bothered by the transvestite be-havior he exhibited. The residents, in contrast, also knew about this person's sexual advances to other males but were far more outraged by his wearing of women's clothing. When he would appear in the common room at Gatewood "in drag" he would be greeted by laughter, catcalls, and shouts of "faggot." His lack of recognition of group norms and his failure to give up his deviant behavior had several con-sequences for his relations with others. He became such a marginal member of the community that he spent very little time at Gatewood, reducing his waking time there to a few meals a week, during which he avoided contact with other residents. When he took meals at Gate-wood he was found by himself, facing the wall. Residents made fewer efforts to bring him back into line but did spend a good deal of time ridiculing him when he was present. The norms of identity and action which defined the appropriate characteristics of group members did

not include transvestism, which was known about by all and was nega-
tively evaluated.

Not all forms of sexual deviance were unacceptable to the residents. One male resident was prone to expose his genitalia in public,
generally in the vicinity of Gatewood. While the staff were concerned
about the reaction of neighbors to these public displays and particularly for the safety of the exposer, should he have become regarded as
a threat to neighborhood women and children, the residents were generally tolerant of him. On one occasion he walked out into the cor-
ridors of Gatewood completely nude, but outside of the immediate
uproar this caused, he was not ridiculed on other occasions when he
was appropriately dressed.

The development of informal group norms and their informal
means of enforcement described above also permitted the mental
health therapy aides to spend more of their time instructing residents
in areas of personal grooming, hygiene and dress. Aides were less
involved in breaking up fights between residents and less the target
of abuse when residents were responding to their peers' expectations
for appropriate behavior.

As time went on, the staff generally became less concerned with
internal coordination between residents and with restricting access
to regions where work was conducted. They did remain involved in efforts to get residents to communicate responsibly to staff as far as
their outside activities were concerned. While staff did not attempt to
regulate outside activities of residents, except where some scheduled mass activity was involved, they did try to persuade residents
not to go out at night, to avoid certain regions of the neighborhood
where there was some trafficking in drugs, and to stay away from
bars and even from the purchase of alcoholic beverages.

The residents' responsibility also involved anticipation that
staff required information about self-directed outside activities. Their
daily round of life shifted to a most conventional rhythm; they went
out to work each day, and returned. Because of this, the staff was
less in a position to observe activities outside Gatewood. Consequently
they became more concerned with inculcating responsible behavior.
The staff insisted that residents who went to relatives for weekends
tell the staff of their plans; that telephone calls be made to Gatewood
if a resident would be late in returning from work or entertainment;
that residents arrive back in the evening at a reasonable hour or if
they were going out for several hours that they notify the office.

In conclusion, a system of social organization evolved, starting
from the basic problem of regulating Gatewood as a managed residence in which residents had established a number of points of contact with the larger community. Social regulation developed not only
through ongoing interaction between staff and residents and among

fellow residents, but also through attempts at problem-solving involved in the residents learning how to get along with each other, and with the staff. The more residents were able to find other social roles in the community, particularly through the social network available at the sheltered workshops, the more staff were limited to primary instructional tasks related to individual adaptation to the larger community; for example, personal appearance and grooming, or learning how to get around in the city on public transportation. Consequently, staff authority in the lives of residents, exercised widely during the first six months, later became limited to personal counseling activities and referral and tracking functions, in which members had some obligations to staff and to each other.

The informal community development which took place among residents: (1) identified deviance; (2) expressed collective evaluations of the actors; and (3) led to efforts on the part of residents to deal with deviance, both in sponsored group counseling sessions and through their own informal mechanisms of social control. Out of these efforts emerged an implicit definition of community membership, based on participation in these efforts to develop shared norms of identity and action; at the same time, efforts to deal with transgressors promoted group solidarity.

These developments, finally, produced a social division of labor in which staff and residents became aware of the differences in social networks in which they participated as well as of their common linkage to Gatewood. In the next chapter, questions related to the response of individual mentally retarded adults to this social organization will be examined.

REFERENCE

Goffman, Erving
    1961   Asylums: Essays on the Social Situations of Mental Patients and Other Inmates. New York: Anchor Books.

Given the characteristics of social life at state schools presented
in Chapter Two, one might conclude that relocation at Gatewood was a
desired change, or that the choice of relocation was always clear cut.
However, since residents had lived in state schools for the better part
of their lives, opportunities to move on to better living quarters and
the possibility of employment in a vocational rehabilitation sheltered
workshop represented at the same time both an exciting and frighten-
ing change. While none of the respondents expected that they would
live at a community residence at this time in their lives, many were
responsive to being closer to their families, and wished to live at home
again. Some potential candidates for Gatewood appeared very surprised when interviewed, and one person said that "I thought that the
only way I would ever get out of here is in a pine box." Other candidates, who had been moved from closed to open wards at state schools,
saw community relocation as an extension of their past progress.

When a team of mental health workers appeared at the state
schools to screen eligible candidates for Gatewood, some residents
were resigned rather than overjoyed at the prospect of leaving the
state school. One attendant reported that the mentally retarded
women she cared for had had experience with unexpected transfers
from ward to ward. In general, the staff on the wards where screening was carried out resented the favorable publicity given to community-based residential facilities and the invidious comparisons
made in the mass media between state schools and new facilities. It
was observed that state school personnel downplayed the relocation
program and the social differences between facilities and, accordingly,
may have understated the advantages of relocation to the retarded
adults whom they prepared for screening visits.

Informal communication about Gatewood had indeed preceded
the visit of the resettlement team. State school patients not only knew

of the location of the facility but regarded it as a foregone conclusion that the "bright" and less troublesome residents were going to be moved out. Screening was only the first step in the process, but it was regarded as having some finality. Despite guarded comments by the resettlement team, many of the mentally retarded adults who were interviewed considered the decision to transfer them already made, and certainly out of their hands.

A few residents at state schools who were employed in day work off the grounds of these large institutions were quite reluctant to leave. Some people who were already living in the best buildings or who participated in sheltered workshop programs off the grounds refused to leave the institution, or even visit Gatewood. Others resisted movement from the state schools more indirectly. Some individuals who were scheduled to visit Gatewood could not be found on the day they were to make the trip, and others cried when waiting reluctantly to be interviewed by the team in charge of resettlement screening.

Upon visiting Gatewood, prospective residents began to ask questions about the extent to which currently achieved privileges could be maintained. Men were very much concerned about whether they would be allowed to travel on their own. Women were rarely asked such questions about outside activities, having rarely been granted the right to go off the grounds of the state schools without escort. Constant comparisons were made by the women between their current living quarters and Gatewood because some of the female candidates for resettlement lived at the state school in a model building in which rooms were already shared with only one other person. Prospective residents at Gatewood admired the newness of the facility and its appointments, but were most astonished by its noninstitutional character. One resident noted that the windows were free of the heavy metal screening characteristically found on state school buildings for the protection of residents. Sometimes the difference in size and appearance between the two facilities confused potential residents. One person asked where the dining hall was located while actually standing in Gatewood's dining area, far smaller than that in the state school.

RESPONSES TO LIVING AT GATEWOOD

How did resettled retarded adults evaluate Gatewood in comparison to a state school? Why did they decide to leave the state school? What did they see as the major advantages and disadvantages of community living? Have their aspirations changed since living at Gatewood?

Upon moving to Gatewood, residents appeared enthusiastic about the facility and some spent a great deal of time calling their parents or calling attendants at state schools, to tell them about their arrival and about the new accommodations The bright and cheerful, home-like surroundings were something which all residents approved of. After living at a community residence for seven to ten months, a distinct improvement in the quality of life was also recognized. These reactions were most evident in answers given during the second interview. Respondents were asked about the things they liked about state schools shortly after their arrival at Gatewood, and about Gatewood after living there from seven to ten months. The freedom and independence of living at a community residence was recognized by almost half the respondents as its most desirable feature. As one person remarked, "There are two to a room here. I can take a bath whenever I want to. I can go to the store whenever I want to."

While almost one-third of the respondents failed to say anything favorable about the state schools (as can be seen in Table 5.1), only 5 percent found that there was nothing they liked about Gatewood. This willingness to name and list the positive features of Gatewood continued to be expressed in interviews conducted fifteen months after relocation.

TABLE 5.1

Percent of Gatewood Residents Naming Favorable
Aspects of State Schools and Gatewood

	Interview		
	I	II	III
Did Respondent	Upon	After	After
Name Any Favorable	Relocation	7-10 Mos.	16-20 Mos.
Aspects of Facility?	(N = 45)	(N = 38)	(N = 41)
Yes	69	95	90
No	31	5	10

Note: For interviews I and II X^2 = 7.26, p < .01, df = 1; for interviews II and III X^2 = .10 (not significant).
Source: Data compiled by the authors.

To what extent were unfavorable aspects of the two facilities mentioned? Negative aspects of the state schools, such as fighting with other residents, poor treatment by staff, and inadequate facilities were mentioned by 94 percent of the respondents, while only 58 percent listed negative aspects of Gatewood, such as fighting with other residents. (These data are not presented in accompanying tables because they are not statistically significant.)

While comparisons between state schools and Gatewood after seven to ten months of community living showed marked shifts in satisfaction, they do not reveal whether respondents felt that the quality of life had remained at the same high level since relocation. As can be seen in Table 5.2, respondents were asked a separate question about their feelings about being at Gatewood. This question was repeated in all interviews and at all times; a majority of the responses were positive. After the second interview, an increase in positive responses of 15 percent and an increase of negative responses of 8 percent were found. Conversely, more neutral comments such as "it's okay" decreased dramatically. Fifteen months after resettlement at Gatewood, the modal response to being there still remained positive. However, results from the third interview indicate a trend toward expression of more neutral statements, which increased 19 percent when compared with results from the second interview.

TABLE 5.2

Percent of Gatewood Residents Expressing
Negative, Neutral, or Positive Attitudes Toward Gatewood

	Interview		
	I	II	III
	Upon	After	After
	Relocation	7-10 Mos.	16-20 Mos.
Type of Attitude	(N = 50)	(N = 48)	(N = 47)
Negative	2	10	15
Neutral	38	15	34
Positive	60	75	51

Note: For interviews I and II X^2 = 8.71, p < .05, df = 2; for interviews II and III X^2 = 6.24, p < .05, df = 2.

Source: Data compiled by the authors.

The shift toward greater neutrality in attitudes toward living at Gatewood may result from increasing desires rather than increased dissatisfaction with community residential living. Given the low correlation between length of time living at Gatewood and positive attitude, it is possible that some respondents have acquired new aspirations for independent living and now consider Gatewood less desirable than in the past. Since the trend is toward neutral rather than negative attitudes toward the residence, this interpretation seems plausible. The subject of aspirations—both those which residents had upon relocation and those acquired since that time—requires a separate and more detailed discussion.

ASPIRATIONS

The major reasons provided for making the transfer to Gatewood were (1) because it was a better place to live, and (2) because it was closer to home. Respondents remained very consistent during the first and second interviews in suggesting that these were the advantages found both in anticipating relocation and after seven to ten months of living at Gatewood. (See Chapter Seven for a discussion of changing relationships with the families of Gatewood residents.)

The third major reason for wanting to be relocated was the desire to go to work. Almost 20 percent of the respondents suggested this was their prime motivation for coming to live at the new facility. The initial experience of the residents, however, was not conducive to realizing their desire. In all cases, placement in vocational rehabilitation sheltered workshops occurred after a six-month period of inactivity at Gatewood.

The failure to fulfill the promise to provide opportunities for learning how to work was not only disappointing to Gatewood residents but may have encouraged them to lose interest in working. The aspirations of residents shifted to accommodate the lack of work in vocational rehabilitation settings. Respondents showed an increased interest in engaging in self-initiated activities such as traveling on their own, and going to local stores, parks, and other locations. When asked what they would like to do while living at Gatewood, 41 percent mentioned these activities the second time as compared with 20 percent the first time. This trend may have resulted both from an increased ability to travel to various outside activities on their own as well as from an adaptation to the lack of work or sponsored activities similar to those found in state schools. Fewer residents mentioned work as their desired activity in the second interview, as compared to the first.

It is important to note that moving from a state school to Gatewood involved for some the disruption of work routines which had been socially rewarding. Many of the residents had acquired a great deal of prestige from successfully performing as helpers in various service shops at the large institutions. Those persons who had supervised jobs were most severely tried by the long period of inactivity at Gatewood prior to receiving vocational training. During the first six months, complaints about the lack of work were made whenever one of the authors visited Gatewood.

Life at the state school had not prepared some of the residents for keeping busy when few activities were available. During the first few months of unemployment, many persons were at a loss to know what to do. The women, who had at first expressed concern about not working, later became less concerned and expressed the traditional view that they were content to stay home while the men went out to work. Men were more likely to go outside for recreation and entertainment, while women were more likely to remain at Gatewood.

Each resident at Gatewood received a monthly allowance in the form of Social Security disability payments for incidentals and clothing, which could be spent as they saw fit. Spending provided something to do during the early months of inactivity. The acquisition and use of toilet articles was of great interest. Residents often inappropriately used up the entire contents of the vials, jars, and cans of bath products in one day. In addition, at the beginning of each month a fad of moviegoing developed, particularly among the male residents, who, singly or in twos and threes, would go off to the neighborhood theaters. Once these funds were exhausted, however, there were few ways of earning money. At a state school with its large staff, car washing was a way of acquiring additional cash. Gatewood has a small staff and a high concentration of able residents who could compete for the limited opportunities to make money by working for staff members.

The change toward self-initiated behavior and the lessening of interest in work may have resulted from changing expectations for Gatewood residents. Most respondents simply did not wish to be inactive. This finding results from answers to a question about whether there were any things they did not wish to do or wished to avoid. The frequency of certain responses to this question did increase over time; four out of five respondents said during the second interview that they wished to avoid inactivity, compared with only slightly more than half during the first interview.

RECOGNITION OF OPPORTUNITIES IN COMMUNITY LIVING

The emphasis on activities was also part of an indirectly articulated desire for new experiences Many of these relocated mentally

retarded adults expressed the sad recognition that they had been kept
away from society for many years and that there are experiences in
the "outside" world to which they had not had access. Travel represents some of the experience that they desire—not just in the sense
of something to do, but also as something which gives one a personal
history and something to talk about. Their past experiences in state
institutions represent deprivation of the highly individualized experience of having been somewhere and been able to take memories away
from the experience. Travel, in contrast, represents independence
and autonomy, and a deepening of oneself as a person who has had a
unique past, as well as one unspoiled by the shame of having been
"put away" or "locked up."

The relocated mentally retarded adults at Gatewood were able
to make several interesting comparisons between the opportunities
available in their new location and those available in state schools.
The majority of their answers focused on their independence and their
freedom to make decisions for themselves at Gatewood.

> Interviewer: Is it different here than at state school?
> Respondent 1: They lock the doors and this and that at state
> school.
> Respondent 2: Here it is better. There they always say where
> are you going and you got to get back on time. If
> you fight and fool around they put you on the
> locked ward. Here they don't.

Some respondents found the state school to be full of conflict.

> Respondent 3: There was too much trouble and everything. So
> many fights and everything like that.
> Respondent 4: I like it here. I don't have the aggravation I had
> with the attendants.

A few respondents conceived of the differences in terms of having a stimulating life and leading a round of life like others in the
community.

> Respondent 5: State school is so dead, you know. You don't go
> out working like most people. You don't go to
> work and everything, yuh know. It's not like that
> at state school. You don't go to the movies, yuh
> know. You can go on the bus like you want to
> (here). Not at state school.

Sometimes the protective environs of institutional living were appreciated, in comparison with the dangers of city life. Increased freedom also signified new responsibilities which often made residents anxious.

> Respondent 6: Up there you have open fields. You have shopping in town. Here you have to watch out for cars.

Later, the same respondent voiced concern about how to manage travel on the mass transit system. This person was not alone in being concerned about travel; other residents told stories of their commuting difficulties and their preferences for using buses rather than trains. These travel problems became less evident as residents became accustomed to the route they used to get to work and return.

Despite these initial difficulties, travel was a desired activity that became available while living at Gatewood. To some residents it meant coming home as well as going away, and telling those whom one has not seen all day about one's adventures. In so doing, the person who travels can also share with others the good feeling of being back in familiar surroundings.

Residents also changed their consumer aspirations after fifteen months at Gatewood. As can be seen in Table 5.3, there was a marked increased interest in saving money when respondents were asked what they would do with $300.00. In addition, fewer responses indicated that residents would have spent their money on nondurable and immediately consumable items such as candy, cigarettes, and soda after fifteen months than when first relocated. Aspirations to save money for such goals as the purchase of a radio or phonograph may be a consequence of the opportunity to earn money.

Response to living at Gatewood varied according to the extent to which residents felt that the staff were providing the services they required to realize their aspirations. Respondents were more likely to report that the staff of the state school provided for their needs than, after seven to ten months of living there, the staff of Gatewood did. At the time of the second interview, residents were just beginning their placement or training in vocational rehabilitation sheltered workshops and may not have perceived the Gatewood staff as benefactors because of the long period of inactivity just completed. In contrast, as can be seen in Table 5.4, residents expressed almost unanimous satisfaction with the Gatewood staff after fifteen months of contact with them.

Finally, a few of the more able residents saw living at a community residence as only a step in the direction of further independence. During the first interview, none of the respondents suggested that they wished to live independently and without supervision. During

TABLE 5.3

Percent of Gatewood Residents Who Would Save, Purchase
Durable or Semidurable Goods, or Purchase
Nondurable Goods If They Had $300.00

	Interview		
	I	II	III
	Upon	After	After
What Respondent Would	Relocation	7-10 Mos.	16-20 Mos.
Do with $300.00	(N = 44)	(N = 45)	(N = 45)
Save the money	7	29	33
Purchase durable or semidurable goods	70	60	64
Purchase nondurable goods	23	11	2

Note: For interviews I and II X^2 = 8.18, p < .05, df = 2; for interviews II and III X^2 = 2.88 (not significant).
Source: Data compiled by the authors.

TABLE 5.4

Percent of Residents Who Reported That Staff
Provided for Their Desires or Needs
at State School and Gatewood

	Interview		
	I	II	III
Did Staff Provide	Upon	After	After
for Wants and	Relocation	7-10 Mos.	16-20 Mos.
Needs of Residents?	(N = 42)	(N = 44)	(N = 43)
Yes	79	55	93
No	21	45	7

Note: For interviews I and II X^2 = 5.54, p < .05, df = 1; for interviews II and III X^2 = 16.56, p < .001, df = 1.
Source: Data compiled by the authors.

the second interview, the question, "What are some of the reasons why you came here?" was repeated and ten respondents mentioned such things as wanting "to get out on my own for good."

Other residents possessed similar aspirations and expressed them in answering other questions.

> Interviewer: How do you feel about being in this place?
> Respondent 2: Well, it's O.K. but I would like to be out on my own. I would like to live in a real good apartment.

The subjective reactions to resettlement of the mentally retarded men and women who went to live at Gatewood were generally approving of their new way of living. As with any change of social and physical environment, other people expect the person to perform new roles. These roles constitute a variety of social experiences previously unavailable to Gatewood residents. The next chapter will be concerned with the extent to which new experiences occurred during the first one and one-half years of Gatewood's existence, and with the aspects of living in which these experiences took place.

Moving from a state school to Gatewood not only involved major changes in living arrangements, but produced new social expectations for the residents. The social arrangements of a metropolitan community create a set of constraints on peoples' behavior which are quite different from those of a large and isolated institution. Activities in state schools are within tightly scheduled "blocks" of time, for "blocks" of people who have common characteristics, such as age, sex, and level of self-care. In the urban community, one is likely to move at one's own pace from one setting and group to another. Consequently, the social skills expected of people in the community are based on a model of the environment which includes many assumptions different from those which are operative at a total institution.

Mentally retarded adults who have lived at state schools have for many years had few chances for learning the social skills used in the community and in more domestic living arrangements. For example, they have had little need to learn how to travel in city streets, conduct themselves in groups of threes or fours, maintain contact with the group while getting places, or learn the types of conduct appropriate for public places. Similarly, sharing a bedroom at Gatewood, rather than having a bed in a ward, is a qualitatively different way to live. The transition in physical and social environments made possible a new way to live, but also revealed the lack of many of the skills needed by former patients.

Behavior encouraged and appropriate in a state school often becomes discouraged and inappropriate at Gatewood. A new resident might use a towel to wipe up the floor after a shower, probably trying to make a good impression on the staff by leaving a neat and tidy room. This would be discouraged at Gatewood, while in a state school, which has its own laundry (as all state schools do), using a towel in this way was of no consequence to the staff, and may even be encouraged.

SOCIAL LIFE AT GATEWOOD

Living at Gatewood made possible new and more demanding personal relationships, involving the cooperation and approval of other residents. Bedrooms for two produced both the sense of having a place one could call one's own and the need to share this place with one other person, including sharing the responsibility for its care. From the start, the concept of "the roommate" was utilized, and residents also began to refer to their quarters as "my room" or "our room." Rooms received a personal touch; pictures were placed on the walls and personal belongings were left on bureaus. Occupants also identified their rooms by placing pictures of sports heroes on the doors, since many residents could not read. Sharing a room also produced some squabbles among roommates, and a number of complaints to the director concerning failure to carry out cleaning. In a few instances, rooms were switched to make roommates more compatible.

An important change in the lives of the retarded men and women was the opportunity for informal cross-sex social contacts. At state schools, even dining halls are sex-segregated, and staff-approved contact between the sexes occurs mainly through sponsored activities such as dances. Covert liaisons do occur between men and women at the state schools, but these are not approved by staff. Living at Gatewood provided opportunities for men and women to dine together, to talk with each other, and to dance when they chose to do these things, making possible a fuller development of cross-sex social relationships. This kind of contact also meant that many of the remarks made to each other could become the basis for further cooperation or conflict. During the first few months, three people who frequently engaged in fighting or menacing the opposite sex were transferred back to a state school.

Most residents seemed to approve of the increased cross-sex contacts. They were defined by the residents as a new experience that encouraged the development of new relationships through courting. It was not uncommon to see men and women petting in the public rooms at Gatewood. One woman was particularly articulate about the desirability of contact with men and also described how she drew attention from the man she desired.

Interviewer: What do you like the most about being here?
Respondent: Well, you mind if I say this? Well, you got the boys and girls together. Where at some of these places we were . . . gee, when I first went to state school, a woman didn't even know what a man was, you know what I mean.

Interviewer: Who do you fool around with (flirt with)?
Respondent: W. I sit on him and say, Oh, I'm sorry I thought that was the chair. I do that with everybody.
Interviewer: Do you do that especially with W.?
Respondent: Yeah. Do you ever hear the expression, "I sit back and hear my brethren purr like kittens?"
Interviewer: No.
Respondent: It means like making a fuss over someone to get them interested in you.
Interviewer: Is that what's happening with you and W.? You're making a fuss over him?
Respondent: Yeah.
Interviewer: You like W.
Respondent: Oh, yeah.

State schools were generally organized on the hospital model, emphasizing continuous care and observation of patients and the availability of a substantial medical and nursing component. Patients were regarded as sick people who could not get better and who could do little for themselves without constant direction. Staffing patterns, designed to provide coverage of wards by attendants according to the number of patients, ignored the need to create social or educational programs and the need to concentrate on developing skills at times when patients were most active. Attendants directed and monitored the day-to-day lives of patients in order to prevent harm or injury and left their charges with little opportunity to run their own lives.

The transition from living in the highly directed environment of a state school to the less structured society of Gatewood involved a greater reliance upon the residents to maintain conformity to the rules. Residents have made efforts to use ridicule, for example, to curb those who act "bossy," a trait which may carry over from days when they cared for less able patients. Some of the residents at Gatewood had been consistently rewarded by staff of the state school for taking care of the less able, and initially they evinced little ability to treat other residents as peers. Since the rate of placement in sheltered workshops has increased, there is less occasion for those who attempt to direct others to do so.

It was anticipated that the change in social environment would not only produce disruptions of prior expectations and the need for greater involvement in informal social control, but would also create more opportunities to get to know fellow residents and become more familiar with them. We compared the residents' social network at the state school with that of Gatewood by asking them who they did things with on various occasions during their daily round of life. Specifically, they were asked about the state school: "Who did you eat

your meals with?'' ''Did you go to the state school store with anybody?'' At the second and third interviews these questions were altered to fit Gatewood. Residents were asked to talk about occasions
or activities rather than about friends, so that they would not give
socially desirable answers. Only when respondents voluntarily mentioned a specific name or introduced the term ''my friend'' to refer
to a specific person in answer to these questions were the answers
so coded. When respondents said they ate with ''everybody,'' ''anybody,'' or ''the other residents,'' their answers were coded separately
from those who mentioned names. Fewer respondents mentioned persons by name or said they ate with friends when asked about whom
they ate meals with at the state school than when answering in reference to Gatewood. While the differences were not statistically significant, it is important to note that residents continued to name specific
dining partners at the same rate during the third interview as the
second (see Table 6.1).

A substantial increase in the number of people named or referred to as friends was found in the answers to a question about going
to local stores with other people in the neighborhood of Gatewood, as
compared with going to the community store on the grounds of state
schools. Being accompanied by aides and attendants to stores was
significantly less frequent at Gatewood. However, as Table 6.2 shows,
during the last interview 34 percent of the respondents said they went
to local shops with fellow residents, as compared to 46 percent at the
second interview. At all times one-third of the respondents said they
went to stores alone.

TABLE 6.1

Percent of Residents Mentioning Names of Persons
Whom They Ate With at State School and Gatewood

	Interview		
	I	II	III
Did Resident Name	Upon	After	After
Specific Persons	Relocation	7-10 Mos.	16-20 Mos.
He Ate With?	(N = 48)	(N = 48)	(N = 46)
Yes	19	33	33
No	81	67	67

Note: For interviews I and II X^2 = 1.95 (not significant); for
interviews II and III X^2 = .02 (not significant).
Source: Data compiled by the authors.

TABLE 6.2

Percent of Residents Mentioning Names of Persons
Who Accompanied Them to PX at State School
and Stores at Gatewood

	Interview		
	I	II	III
Did Resident Name	Upon	After	After
Persons He Went to	Relocation	7-10 Mos.	16-20 Mos.
PX or Store with?	(N = 43)	(N = 46)	(N = 44)
Yes	14	46	34
No	86	54	66

Note: For interviews I and II X^2 = 9.12, p < .01, df = 1; for
interviews II and III X^2 = .81 (not significant).
Source: Data compiled by the authors.

Despite early instances of conflict which led to the return of
three residents to state schools, the general level of conflict appears
to be substantially lower at Gatewood than at the state schools. Mentally retarded adults who were asked about whether they fought with
other residents were less likely to say they did while living at Gatewood. Since the selection process screened out those persons with
lengthy histories of acting out behavior, it comes as no surprise that
fighting is less frequently mentioned by respondents as taking place
at the community residence. Despite this finding, staff expressed a
great deal of concern about conflict at Gatewood. The staff members'
perceptions of conflict may result from their general unfamiliarity
with people who lived in state schools. Violence against members of
the staff was treated more quickly and severely than violence against
fellow residents, often leading to quick transfers back to state institutions. With the help of psychologists from a community retardation
service, the staff did establish counseling groups, in which residents
could learn to express their anger in more socially acceptable forms.
Residents learned how to ask for help from roommates, how to register complaints against others, and how to avoid provocative behavior.
Staff inexperience during the first six months may be responsible for
the frequent transfers back to state schools. Six of the ten returnees
left during this period and five of these six left during the first three
months.

Despite these specific instances when residents and staff had
to learn to deal directly with others, relationships between retarded

adults at Gatewood were generally relaxed. As Table 6.3 shows, residents more frequently said they had fun with friends or other people whom they mentioned specifically by name when asked about Gatewood than when asked about living at state schools. Quite often, respondents mentioned that they enjoyed joking around with friends in the evening or went to different places with their friends.

In general, residents at Gatewood acquired a new relationship with aides, which differed from their previous relationship with staff at state schools. Respondents said they did fewer errands and services for staff at Gatewood than for staff at the state schools (see Table 6.4). Activities such as cleaning, sweeping, and mopping were mentioned by over half the respondents during the first interview, and by slightly over one-third in the second one, which concerned activity at Gatewood. Attendants were likely to give food and cigarettes as a reward to patients at state schools while Gatewood residents mentioned receiving cash for their work. Rewards, however, were far more likely to be utilized at the state schools to get chores accomplished (see Table 6.5). State school attendants were regarded as providing for almost all of the material things needed by respondents.

TABLE 6.3

Percent of Residents Who Named Specific Persons
With Whom They Had Fun at Gatewood and State School

Did Resident Name Persons with Whom He Had Fun?	Interview		
	I Upon Relocation (N = 38)	II After 7-10 Mos. (N = 41)	III After 16-20 Mos. (N = 38)
Yes	8	34	37
No	92	66	63

Note: For interviews I and II $X^2 = 8.04$, $p < .01$, df = 1; for interviews II and III $X^2 = .06$ (not significant).
Source: Data compiled by the authors.

TABLE 6.4

Percent of Residents Who Performed Chores for Aides
at State School and Gatewood

	Interview	
	I	II
Did Resident	Upon	After
Perform Chores	Relocation	7–10 Mos.
for Aides?	(N = 44)	(N = 44)
Yes	57	34
No	43	66

Note: X^2 = 3.71, p < .10, df = 1.
Source: Data compiled by the authors.

TABLE 6.5

Percent of Residents Who Received Any Payment from Aides
for Chores at State School and Gatewood

	Interview	
	I	II
Did Resident	Upon	After
Receive Payment	Relocation	7–10 Mos.
from Aides?	(N = 24)	(N = 13)
Yes	87	46
No	13	54

Note: X^2 = 5.36, p < .05, df = 1.
Source: Data compiled by the authors.

Relations with Gatewood aides were much more informal than relationships with attendants at state schools All Gatewood aides were called by their first name, while almost all state school attendants were referred to as Mr. or Miss. Aides at Greenwood often became fond of particular residents to the point that other residents became quite envious. At several staff meetings the director of the facility pointed out to the aides that they promoted envy among residents and should not become friendly with only a few of them. Since aides were working class women from the neighborhood in which Gatewood was located, some residents visited them at home or encountered them in the neighborhood during non-working hours.

While Gatewood staff were regarded as less materially rewarding by residents than state school staff, they were also far less punitive. Respondents were asked what would happen if they were caught "fooling around" at the state school and at Gatewood. This question was deliberately left vague so that the respondents rather than the interviewer would provide the criteria for deviant behavior. Far fewer residents thought they would be punished for transgressions at Gatewood than at the state school (Table 6.6). Those who did perceive themselves as being subject to punishment at Gatewood mentioned relatively minor punishments, such as being yelled at, as compared with being placed in an isolation room for several days at the state school.

Teasing of residents by staff was frequently mentioned when respondents were asked about life at state schools. In contrast, as Table 6.7 shows, this staff behavior was mentioned less often when questions concerning life at Gatewood were answered.

TABLE 6.6

Percent of Residents Who Reported Being Punished
for Fooling Around

	Interview	
	I	II
Was Resident	Upon	After
Punished for	Relocation	7-10 Mos.
Fooling Around?	(N = 12)	(N = 11)
Yes	17	46
No	83	54

Note: X^2 = 1.09 (not significant).
Source: Data compiled by the authors.

TABLE 6.7

Percent of Residents Who Reported Being Teased
at State School and Gatewood

	Interview		
	I	II	III
	Upon	After	After
Did Resident Report	Relocation	7-10 Mos.	16-20 Mos.
Being Teased?	(N = 48)	(N = 49)	(N = 47)
Yes	56	35	30
No	44	65	70

Note: For interviews I and II X^2 = 4.54, p < .05, df = 1; for
interviews II and III X^2 = .26 (not significant).
Source: Data compiled by the authors.

Social life at Gatewood involved fewer protections and restrictions than existed at a state school. The state school experience had not prepared residents for peer contact under the new living arrangements. The establishment and learning of rules for living and of informal means of control were primary tasks during the period of transition.

Living at Gatewood not only was made more informal, as represented by the physical arrangements and social contacts available between residents and staff; the location of the facility also encouraged the use of community resources. The residents who had experience in using facilities only on the grounds of state schools now had to utilize community-based recreational, vocational, and health facilities.

Gatewood was primarily a domiciliary facility with little program or services available to provide for the social, vocational, or health needs of its residents. An arts and crafts program and a limited educational program were established at the facility, but the major sources of vocational activity and ancillary services would have to be found at other places, including community centers, religious organizations, vocational rehabilitational workshops, medical centers, and hospitals. Right from the start, residents were encouraged to use these institutions in the community. At first, residents were taken by a staff member to an ambulatory medical clinic to receive health care. Later, residents went on their own or in the company of another resident who was capable of independent travel. Similarly, when placement

in sheltered workshops was finally achieved, travel was again independent or done in the company of a resident who could see to it that
other workshop trainees from Gatewood arrived and returned safely.
Residents occasionally were lost or were separated on subways or
buses, but for the most part the travel program worked well. Some
residents took great pride in the fact that they were able to travel by
themselves on a complicated mass transit system while others were
pleased that they were able to help others get from place to place.
This separation between domicile and workplace not only encouraged
residents to utilize the community for services but also encouraged
them to go outside of Gatewood for entertainment and recreation. Consequently local community centers and other facilities were used for
sports and pursuit of hobbies. The sheltered workshop also became
an important source of social relationships for trainees, a point to
which we will shortly return.

The mentally retarded, like those who are not mentally retarded,
must establish their right to be present in public places by learning
appropriate social skills. Social competency involves being able to put

other people in public places at their ease. This set of skills may take several forms, including ways of showing that one's intentions are harmless and that one is in control of oneself. For the mentally retarded adult such behavior might also involve giving a good account of one's actions, perhaps even by revealing that one is mentally retarded. However, such announcements can be made at appropriate and/or inappropriate times. Recognizing the situational character of accounts or explanations is an important social skill in any person's repertoire and helps him to make a good impression. Bringing attention to a disability is something that handicapped people do ordinarily in order to help put the non-handicapped at their ease in face-to-face interaction. This ritual of interaction has been designated as "deviance disavowal" by Fred Davis (1964) and is utilized by the handicapped to help normalize relationships with others who are similarly situated.

Many former state school patients had not learned how to act as ordinary, competent pedestrians. If they are with other people, they have to demonstrate to strangers that they are by maintaining symbolic contact with their companions. Similarly, if they are alone in a public place, they may draw a great deal of attention by staring or looking purposeless, particularly if they look different in physical appearance, dress, or demeanor. As a result of this devalued behavior, others may challenge their right to be present. Retarded adults clustered together in large numbers can be attention-getting in themselves because they are unusual, particularly if they are with a person who is "in charge of them," reinforcing the idea that they cannot take care of themselves. Finally, by depending on a leader, they may not learn the skills necessary to use the streets.

Community living meant not only getting used to a more informally organized environment but also learning to get services and take care of other needs within the city. No longer under benevolent protection, residents had to let others know what they needed, and that they knew how to get it.

WORKING IN THE COMMUNITY

The workplace functioned to maintain existing relationships as well as to establish new relationships. The separation of home from workplace for these Gatewood residents is not as extreme as it is for other people in the community who work. As many as ten people from Gatewood were in training at a single workshop. Most respondents said that they ate their lunch at the workshop with other people from Gatewood. Still, the workshop was a place where respondents claimed to find new boyfriends and girlfriends; eight residents claimed to have met them at the workshop they attended (Table 6.8).

TABLE 6.8

Percent of Residents Whose Boyfriends or Girlfriends
Were Residents or Nonresidents of State School or Gatewood

	Interview		
	I	II	III
Residential Status	Upon	After	After
of Boy or	Relocation	7-10 Mos.	16-20 Mos.
Girlfriend	(N = 22)	(N = 27)	(N = 27)
Resident	95	56	52
Nonresident	5	44	48

Note: For interviews I and II X^2 = 7.95, p < .01, df = 1; for
interviews II and III X^2 = 0.00 (not significant).
Source: Data compiled by the authors.

Pride in accomplishment in work was evident in responses to
questions concerning how jobs were acquired, whether trainees felt
they were doing a good job, and whether they enjoyed their work. Opportunity for steady work provided benchmarks or ways for respondents to recognize and measure their personal progress as well as
their ability, as is illustrated in the following interviews. Here, for
example, three workshop trainees talk about different levels of achieve-
ment in their work experience:

Interviewer: How did you get the job?
Respondent: The first job I got was in a workshop. You do a
test first. After the test you go to a metal job. I
worked there for three weeks, then I got out of
there.
Interviewer: How come you got out of there?
Respondent: Well, they think I was good.

* * *

Interviewer: Do you do a good job?
Respondent: I'm doing good. I know it. I know it. I know I'm
doing three pounds of metal. I know I'm doing
good.

* * *

Interviewer: What do you do?
Respondent: I bend metal.

Interviewer: Do you like it?
Respondent: Yeah.

The experience of attending a workshop also provides some residents with something to talk about when they return in the evening. Residents were observed conversing about some of the features of their respective workshops, with particular interest paid to the different vending machines. Other people at Gatewood discussed the different kinds of jobs they have done at workshops or complained about not getting the job they wanted. Even getting lost in the transit system while traveling to and from their jobs has become a topic of conversation on occasion. Working, then, is a new experience which is conducive to expanding the number of social contacts of the respondent as well as to expanding the experiences which can be related to others at Gatewood.

The work experience has also become a source of great pride for people who were seldom regularly paid for work at state schools or who were provided with tips, often in the form of food or cigarettes. Residents returning to Gatewood with checks in the modest amounts of $5.00 to $10.00 per week took great pleasure in being able to earn money. Money is now far more important in their lives, since there are a variety of places to spend it, and purchases are not restricted to what is available at the state schools' community stores. In fact, when asked "What would you do if you had $300.00?" respondents were far more likely, during the second interview, as compared with the first, to say they wanted semidurable consumer items which they could now afford, such as radios and tape recorders. Residents could now save up for those purchases, whereas at state schools such desires were not as realizable. During the first interview there was somewhat more emphasis on consumables such as candy or cigarettes, but these differences were not statistically significant.

The intrinsic nature of the work experience is quite different from what was previously experienced at state schools. Assembly work at benches and tables is far more disciplined in the sheltered workshop than at state schools. The programs focus on increasing the trainees' attention span and capacity to follow instructions, as well as on providing specific skills in assembly and packing tasks. Significantly, far more respondents said they could not talk to each other at work when at sheltered workshops than at state schools (Table 6.9). Trainees at workshops were also less likely to be permitted to get up from their work and get necessary materials and tools than they were at state schools.

Finally, the work experience creates expectations about how well the task was done. Sheltered workshop supervisors are far more concerned with day-to-day evaluation and long-run predictive trends

TABLE 6.9

Percent of Residents Who Reported That They Could Talk
While Working at State School and Gatewood

	Interview	
	I	II
Could Resident	Upon	After
Talk While	Relocation	7–10 Mos.
Working?	(N = 37)	(N = 38)
Yes	76	40
No	24	60

Note: X^2 = 8.61, p < .01, df = 1.
Source: Data compiled by the authors.

in performance than are personnel at state schools. Given their goal
of work as a source of rehabilitation, it is no surprise that they are
concerned with these questions of productivity and quality of performance. The workshop experience provides the trainee with a sense that
the activities he is expected to perform are serious. Trainees are
paid on a piece-rate basis and if output is unsatisfactory they receive
less pay or no pay. Given the important place money now occupies in
the lives of these retarded people, the evaluation received from workshop counselors and supervisors can be of central concern.

Vocational rehabilitation programs were organized to transmit
the habit of work as well as skills. Work was structured to simulate the
environment of competitive employment, where standards of performance would have to be met if persons in training were to keep their
jobs. While the tasks performed in sheltered workshops are geared
to the abilities of the trainees, a serious atmosphere prevails, in
order to encourage concentration. Everyone, including those persons
who are not expected to keep up productivity so as to qualify for competitive employment, is trained in following the rules of the workplace and is expected to meet the role requirement of a trainee. Staying at an assigned place was one habit imparted to trainees.

Interviewer: Do you work?
Respondent: Yes.
Interviewer: What do you do?
Respondent: I stay at the table at which the man put me.

Interviewer: What kind of work is it?
Respondent: You know, these needles with the cards in them?
We put the needles through the cards and thread.

Training in a vocational rehabilitation setting approximated the
atmosphere of the world of work, including all the details of arrival,
departure, and starting the day. Most importantly, learning how to
work with others in a cooperative manner was stressed in the program
along with the acquisition of specific skills. Working with others
sometimes was shown to involve interdependency as well as the companionship depicted in the following description:

Well, we wait out there on the fifth floor. They open the
doors. Then each one punches the time clock. Then you
get a sheet of paper, either white, blue or yellow. That
tells you what you are going to work on. You work on
needles. Someone else puts them in, we take them out.

Work may be considered, then, to constitute a central interest
of the Gatewood residents once they are located at a community residence and placed in a vocational rehabilitation sheltered workshop.
Work also becomes a way of creating responsibility among residents
for increased control over their own lives. Personal decision-making
is encouraged by the new responsibilities demanded by attending the
sheltered workshop programs.

Work provides a new orientation to the consequences of their
own actions, providing a more self-reliant way to live. Respondents
frequently reported that attendants hit patients in state schools. In
answer to the question "What happens if you want to stay in bed late
in the morning at a state school?" over half the respondents said
that they would be hit, have water thrown on them or be tossed out of
bed (Table 6.10). In contrast, no respondent mentioned physical punishment if such a situation occurred at Gatewood. Over half of the
respondents said they would be late for work if they stayed in bed in
the morning. A similar finding results when respondents are asked
"What would happen if you want to stay up late?" At the second interview, 22 percent reported that they would be late for work the
next morning, while no such answers were presented when living at
state schools was discussed (Table 6.11). At the third interview only
12 percent reported personal consequences. Residents seemed to
perceive their situation as being free of either organizational or personal constraints, with 60 percent saying nothing could happen if they
stayed up late at night.

TABLE 6.10

Percent of Residents Who Reported Consequences
of Staying in Bed Late at State School and Gatewood

	Interview	
	I	II
	Upon	After
Consequences of Staying	Relocation	7–10 Mos.
in Bed Late	(N = 43)	(N = 45)
No negative consequences (staying in bed late permitted)	9	18
Personal consequences incurred (late for work, miss breakfast)	16	64
Staying in bed late incurs punishment	74	18

Note: $X^2 = 29.14$, $p < .001$, df = 2.
Source: Data compiled by the authors.

TABLE 6.11

Percent of Residents Who Reported Consequences
of Staying Up Late at State School and Gatewood

	Interview		
	I	II	III
	Upon	After	After
Consequences of Staying	Relocation	7–10 Mos.	16–20 Mos.
Up Late	(N = 38)	(N = 45)	(N = 40)
No negative consequences (staying up late permitted)			
Personal consequences incurred (late for work, miss breakfast)			
Staying up late either not permitted, or punished			

Note: For interviews I and II $X^2 = 9.93$, $p < .01$, df = 2; for
interviews II and III $X^2 = 3.15$ (not significant).
Source: Data compiled by the authors.

In summary, the new experience of working and living in the community created many opportunities to become more self-reliant and interdependent with those similarly situated. In the next chapter, the question of old relationships and dependencies will be discussed when the family and its reaction to community living is examined. In addition, the ways in which residents altered these relationships and developed potential substitutes will be considered.

REFERENCE

Davis, Fred
     1964   "Deviance Disavowal: The Management of Strained
              Interaction by the Visibly Handicapped," in Howard S.
              Becker, ed., The Other Side, pp. 119-37. New York:
              The Free Press of Glencoe.

The mentally retarded adults who returned to the community often wished to be located closer to their families. Yet the families of these men and women had voluntarily, albeit perhaps reluctantly, placed them in state facilities many years ago. Few of these parents ever anticipated that their children would return to community living and some parents did not approve of the move. Few parents attempted to take their children back into their homes on a permanent or trial basis.

Parents who placed their children in large and isolated state schools often did so because of the unavailability of day programs and/or local residential programs in the community. Programs for retarded persons beyond school age were virtually nonexistent until the late 1950s and parents often were faced with the problem of what to do with their retarded children when schooling was terminated. State school records were not always complete as to the reasons for placement. This information was unavailable in almost half the cases. When information was available, two reasons were frequently found: the child was unmanageable at home; and/or parents feared for the child's safety in the community.

The majority of placements were made at a time when public schooling for the mentally retarded came to an end. At the time of placement, the school system of the city in which Gatewood is located legally terminated mentally retarded pupils at the age of 16. Since then, the state education law has been altered to require school for disabled pupils from the age of five to twenty-one. Given these additional years of education, it may be anticipated that placement in state schools if now made would take place at a later age. However, because community services and programs are still inadequate to meet the needs of the mentally retarded at all stages in their life cycle, placement in residential care still goes on.

Parents were genuinely surprised by the possibility that their children would be resettled in the community. At the time of the original placement in state schools, many parents had become convinced that their children could not live in the community. In the period of time from placement to the time when they were contacted about Gatewood, many parents had moved from the original area of the city in which they had lived when their retarded children were institutionalized. Since the time of placement many parents had moved away and resettlement for their retarded children would produce no major conveniences for parents. In some cases, parents could not be located at all.

Contact between family and residents was not always maintained during the years of living at the large and isolated public institutions. For some residents, the death of parents also brought to a halt all contact with the outside world.

Interviewer: Do your people come visit you?
Respondent: I got two brothers and sisters. My mother and father died. I don't know where they are. They come see me.
Interviewer: Do you ever go visit them?
Respondent: I don't know where they live.

Parents of children at state schools rarely worked for the development of community services and programs. Rather understandably, their involvement, often limited to a few parents, was in improving facilities at the state institution. Some parents worked in the various benevolent societies at state institutions while others worked through statewide organizations for the help of the mentally retarded. Parents who were active in these organizations often resented efforts to create new institutions in the community and preferred that funds be channeled to upgrade the quality of care at state schools. They quite often felt that their children who were left behind in residential institutions would suffer from this new emphasis on community programs.

Still, many parents immediately saw the advantages of having their children relocated in a new facility rather than being forced to live in the overcrowded and rundown dormitories of the state schools. Upon visiting Gatewood, many of the parents were impressed by the pleasantness of the building, rather than by the location in the community. There were many reservations expressed about having their children moved from the protective environment found at state schools, despite the recent evidence presented on television concerning cruelty and neglect of the mentally retarded who lived there.

INITIAL REACTIONS OF FAMILIES

Many of the parents who visited Gatewood before consenting to allow their children to move there seemed very anxious about this decision, which seemed as monumental as the original decision to place their children at state schools. Neither the team of mental health workers nor the director of the facility anticipated these concerns and were not able to deal with them once presented. From the point of view of the staff, the parents' visit to Gatewood and its pleasant physical environment would surely convince them of the merits of a simple transfer. From the point of view of the parents, particularly those who had organized their lives quite differently since their children went to live at state schools, resettlement in the community had many disadvantages.

Most interesting was the concern expressed about whether residents would be permitted to visit their parents on their own. Some parents expressed disbelief that their children could travel independently while others simply did not wish to have their retarded children call on them. Perhaps in the latter instances parents were reluctant to let it be known to friends and neighbors that they had a mentally retarded child.

In some cases where the parents were deceased, brothers and sisters were now the legally responsible guardians and were even more reluctant to act to change the situation for their retarded siblings. In general, none of the guardians anticipated that their mentally retarded relatives would ever return to community living, particularly in a residential program which involved so little in the way of day-to-day supervision and in which the dangers of the streets would be ever-present.

Some parents openly questioned the advisability of having their children out in the community because of past problems of safety. Others felt that the seizures that some of their children had required continued supervision in an environment in which medical help was immediately available. The question of sexual conduct was also raised in reference to the presence of males and females living in the same building. This concern about sexual activity was not an imaginary one, as several women who were either relocated or considered for relocation at Gatewood were already mothers, with most pregnancies occurring while the women were living at state schools.

Finally, disbelief was also expressed when the director of Gatewood said that all of those living in the facility would go out to work in community-based programs, and receive other services in the community as well. When parents asked about visiting, the director stressed this change in the image of their children: "We want to limit

relatives to night and weekend visits. Think of the residents as working people who have no time during the week to see you. . . ."

CHANGING RELATIONSHIPS

During the first days at Gatewood, residents were visited by
relatives far more often than they visited them. Parents were curious
about how their children were faring in an environment much less
protected than the one they had just left. Increasingly, residents, particularly the males, learned to travel the bus and subway routes to
their parents' homes. This made visiting parents an independent activity, and it also meant that they might enter into a more adult relationship with their families than before, insofar as residents could
have something to say about when they would visit their parents.
Moreover, as the director pointed out, since residents now had access
to the community, parents could not just appear at Gatewood as they
could at the state school and expect to find their children there. Parents were now forced to make arrangements to see the residents,
which gave the residents a new source of responsibility and self-
respect.
    Many from Gatewood spent their weekends at their parents'
homes; visiting also took place at Gatewood, mainly on weekends.
However, in contrast, contact with patients left behind or transferred
to other places has not been kept up.
    Over the first seven to ten months of living at Gatewood, no
change was found in the frequency of visiting parents in their homes
and a significant reduction in receiving visits was found (see Table
7.1). However, a substantial increase in the number of those who reported that they were able to travel to visit their families by themselves was reported in the second interview. The increased capacity
to travel independently may produce more frequent reports of visiting
parents, particularly as the parents become older or as other residents become able to travel independently. It is not unreasonable to
expect that the Gatewood residents may begin to act more independently and, in turn, be treated more as adults by their parents as they
begin to earn money and travel on their own. Those residents who
learned how to get to their parents' homes were also at an advantage
in comparison to other residents, insofar as they could learn to travel
independently to other places as well. Linkage with one's family was
not only an advantage emotionally, but provided greater access to the
community as well. Residents were generally pleased that they could
get to their parents' homes by themselves by walking or using public
transportation, as illustrated by the following interview:

TABLE 7.1

Percent of Residents Receiving Visits from Family
While Living at State School and Gatewood

	Interview		
	I	II	III
	Upon	After	After
Did Resident's	Relocation	7-10 Mos.	16-20 Mos.
Family Visit?	(N = 51)	(N = 49)	(N = 48)
Yes	88	67	58
No	12	33	42

Note: For interviews I and II X^2 = 5.19, p < .05, df = 1; for
interviews II and III X^2 = .50 (not significant).
Source: Data compiled by the authors.

Interviewer: Do you ever go visit your people?
Respondent: I go by myself. I know where it is now. I don't
            need nobody to take me home. I go by myself.
Interviewer: Did you go by yourself when you lived at state
            school?
Respondent: No.

This pattern of visiting parents at their homes may be inferred
from the 30 percent reduction of visits by parents to Gatewood that
had occurred by the time of the third interview.

While it is not evident that residents have become closer to their
families in an emotional as well as a physical sense or are more involved with them, there are still significant occasions when residents
and their families do get together. Over half the residents who had
families went to their homes for Thanksgiving in 1973. A majority of
the residents also said they had celebrated their last birthday with
their families. On the first and second anniversaries of Gatewood,
an open house celebration was held in honor of the residents. Family
attendance and participation was very substantial and residents took
great pleasure in introducing both residents and staff to their families.
Sadly, those who did not have visitors on these days were at a loss for
what to do and seemed to feel left out.

Many residents have lost contact with parents over the years
for such reasons as death, retirement and resettlement in places like
Florida and California, occupational mobility requiring relocation of

one's home, ethnic group relocation from the original area of settlement as immigrants or migrants, or from lack of interest or years of
difficulty in getting together. It may be entirely unrealistic to expect
that residents and their relatives will immediately (or ever) see each
other more frequently than in the past. What is interesting is the way
in which residents have invited other residents to visit their mothers
and fathers, either for a weekend or for dinner. This behavior represents a new form of relating to their peers as well as to their parents.

Similarly, every evening in the public rooms of Gatewood, the
different corners become closed circles in which residents sit and
talk or watch television. The same areas are utilized night after night
by the same people, many of whom sit around in their bathrobes and
pajamas, snacking and passing the time. Such identified groups constitute primary peer groups, which are appropriate functional equiva-
lents of kinship ties for adults.

Groups seemed to develop among those relocated from the same
state school, perhaps because these residents already knew each other
or because of the common experience of being transferred at the same
time. When residents named the persons with whom they ate meals or
went to local stores, there was strong preference for people from the
same state schools. Residents also reported helping each other in
such tasks as grooming, particularly when a person had some physical
disability which made it difficult to complete an activity. In general,
there seemed to be great pleasure taken in assisting the less able,
provided that it could be seen why the person needed help.

Residents who were part of informal social groups looked out
for each other in other ways. One incident, reported by an older man
who was part of a group of three Jewish males who were from the
same institution, reveals how this concern becomes almost paternal:

> M. mentioned to me that N., L., and he were asked to help
> push a car to a gas station. After completing this chore
> they were offered a six-pack of beer for their effort. M.
> said he had to stop N. from accepting it and asked the
> owner of the car if he could give them money instead. The
> owner of the car gave each one of them fifty cents. M. was
> very pleased by what he did. I asked M. if he could drink
> beer and he said that he could but that he didn't want to
> do it with N. around. He felt that N. was too young and
> couldn't handle it.

In conclusion, there is evidence that greater independence is
manifested in the residents' relationship with their families and that
many of the initial reservations expressed by parents have been over-

come. Further evidence of increased independence and expression of choice will be discussed in the following chapter.

What is interesting and exciting to report, because it is evidence of integration at Gatewood, is the increasing reliance on familial surrogates, largely those developed among the residents themselves and without the help of the staff. These peer groups are not exclusively sex-segregated, and operate independent of staff, despite a kind of forced familiarization attempted by the staff, particularly by one housekeeping couple who demanded to be treated like parents. The more egalitarian peer group units developed by the residents themselves seemed more in keeping with the organizational character of Gatewood, preserving their newly acquired autonomy and preventing the substitution of a new inauthentic way of acting for the inauthentic way of acting previously learned at the state schools.

Some of these relationships have become the basis of new commitments and responsibilities. While many residents said that they desired to leave the state school in order to live closer to their parents, some literally wanted to return to their parents' homes. However, after two years of living at Gatewood, some of these residents no longer wished to return to their parents' homes, but considered living at Gatewood preferable to living with their parents. Gatewood represents a source of continuous care and support, while living at home is always hedged by the continued uncertainty produced by the possibility of the death of one's parents. As is shown in one set of comments, the residents were very much concerned about their future. The family also can mean greater conflict, and separation from friends and loved ones found at Gatewood:

> I told my mother I don't want to go home for good because if I go home for good it give me headache . . . too much trouble. I get sick and I want to kill myself if I go home. I went home and I knocked things off the table. I went into the bathroom to calm down. I said leave me alone I calm down my ownself. I came back and I told the doctor I no wanna go home. I only want to go home on vacation and come back. That was it. How, if I go home and my mother pass away then I be stuck. There would be nobody then to take care of me. . . .I got to take care of my girl. My girl ain't got nobody. I take care of her. I give my money to her and all that. I got to take care of her. She ain't got nobody.

In conclusion, it can be seen that the boundaries between those who are family and those who are fellow residents seem to be less distinctively drawn by residents as they become familiar with living with others. Residents have learned to take care of others and to be taken care of by others with whom they live or for whom they have affection, not simply with those who are legally responsible for them or are paid to take care of them. The family may become not just a private resource, but an experience to share with those who are needy. In turn, the peer group may become regarded as the source of identity and protection because of the choices involved and the responsibilities incurred. In the next chapter, the related questions of the extent, direction and shaping of responsibility and self-determination will be discussed.

8

RESPONSIBILITY AND
SELF-RELIANCE

Most of the mentally retarded adults discussed in this study were placed in state schools because it was believed that there were no other alternatives to residential care. Parents believed that their children could not take care of themselves and were better off in protective surroundings. Placement at a state school was considered as an improvement over either staying home with little to do and with no adult supervision, or being exposed to the dangers of urban life. It is significant that the mean age of placement (15.7 years) at state schools is close to the age at which schooling was terminated for the mentally retarded in public schools in the 1950s. Since the time of placement, many community-based facilities have been established that provide day programs, mainly in the area of vocational rehabilitation in sheltered workshops. While the number of placements available in these programs is not adequate to meet the need, current expert opinion and state policy sees placement in residential care as the last resort, or something to be used where alternative forms of care are unavailable.

After living in a large and isolated state school for fifteen years or more, inmates generally lose whatever adaptive and social skills needed for self-care that they may have possessed, particularly the ability to travel independently. State schools can be characterized as custodial institutions, partly because of the kind of care received and partly because little effort is usually made to train and prepare people for return to more independent ways of living. Rehabilitation was rarely a goal of large and isolated institutions; persons in state schools hardly ever left. Some of the residents at Gatewood remarked that the state schools were "easy to get into but hard to get out of."

The programs of large and isolated residential institutions were designed to retain people rather than to rehabilitate them. Staff resources at such facilities were allocated to achieve that goal, with few resources set aside to promote a return to community living. When a retarded child, adolescent, or adult was "put away," there was little expectation on the part of staff that he would be returned to his former community. It is reasonable to expect that Gatewood residents, having adapted to institutional life, would have some difficulties in adjusting to a new way of living. While they were still considered wards of the state while living at Gatewood, much had changed in the way in which they could exercise control over their lives.

The social situations of these ex-patients were altered by their removal from large and isolated state schools and by the new experiences involved in placement at Gatewood. In a sense, necessity changed their status from total dependence to limited independence: residents of Gatewood were considered capable of using the community for entertainment, able to travel, or capable of being taken to a sheltered workshop by another resident who could travel. This process of redefinition took place even though residents received no special training in these areas of community living.

The effective pressure on the staff of Gatewood to encourage access to the community had several sources, not the least of which was the clear lack of alternative programs within the facility, the lack of space for such programs, and the lack of funds to pay for staff to run them. In addition, outside supervisory agencies were also opposed to the centralization of all services at the residential location, an arrangement which would lead to the re-creation of social isolation within the community, albeit on a smaller scale than found at state schools. Finally, the cost of maintaining a mentally retarded person in the community could be lower than the cost of residential care if wherever possible existing services were utilized, rather than having them created expressly for the mentally retarded.

By virtue of this objective problem faced by the staff of Gatewood, residents were encouraged to find things to do in the community. There were many opportunities for new experiences in the social and physical environment of the city, particularly in the areas of recreational and vocational activities, including learning new skills and meeting other people. Residents began to rely very heavily on the community for these activities, and much of the responsibility for finding and choosing activities was left to them. Indeed, as was reported in Chapter Five, aspirations for self-initiated activities increased, along with the increased opportunity for such activities.

With the larger world outside of Gatewood fast becoming the location for their daily round of life, the community also came to be regarded as a place where residents could realize their aspirations. These goals went beyond merely looking to the community for work and recreation; residents hoped to eventually live there much like ordinary citizens. A small number of residents who traveled independently and who were doing well as workshop trainees (and who were models of adjustment at Gatewood as well), began to show interest in moving into a more independent residential setting. One person thought he would like to get his own apartment because he thought he was able to cook and do housework. Another resident was interested in finding a roommate with whom he could share an apartment. (An apartment living program has been established by the regional offices of the state developmental agency which provides quarters for "graduates" from Gatewood.)

While fewer than 10 percent of the residents expressed interest in apartment living, almost everyone developed relations with Gatewood staff which were more independent than those they had entered into with staff at state schools. The "benevolent shelter" which characterized the state schools and the concomitant ways in which retarded adults depended on attendants did not prevail at Gatewood. In addition, many of the day-to-day decisions at state schools which resulted from tight scheduling of activities involving blocks of people, such as bedtime hours, were handled more flexibly at Gatewood.

Respondents were asked questions concerning who made decisions about bedtime hours and the time to get up in the morning. In both cases, respondents reported they now were much more likely to make these decisions themselves than they had been at state schools (see Table 8.1). Similarly, other decisions were now more in the hands of residents, including decisions about when to get haircuts and when to take showers. These differences continued to be significant at the time of the third interview. Their new work roles were a central concern to many residents. Personal decision-making was encouraged by their realization that they had to get to work and be able to carry out their assignments. Work, as was shown in Chapter Six, was a way of organizing the lives of residents, enabling self-regulation to take place, and replacing an imposed order established in the wards of state schools.

Residents were not permitted to be responsible for all aspects of self-care at Gatewood. While they were encouraged to use vacuum cleaners and lawn mowers, other appliances necessary for self-care were not available to them. Consequently, residents were not able to learn how to use such more delicate and expensive machines as washing machines and dryers. While a washing machine and dryer were available at Gatewood, use was limited to staff or to only one or two residents, who did the laundry for the entire population. The budget-conscious owner and director of Gatewood did not want to risk damage to these appliances, and strict limitations were set up about who was permitted to use them. Residents were also not instructed in how to

TABLE 8.1

Percent of Residents and Staff Making Decisions Regarding Scheduling and Personal Hygiene

Decision and Decision Makers	I Upon Relocation	II After 7-10 Mos.	III After 16-20 Mos.	x^2 For Interviews: I - II	II - III
Who decides what time the resident goes to bed?	(N = 43)	(N = 50)	(N = 46)	17.53^a	$.87^c$
Resident	12	56	67		
Staff	88	44	33		
Who decides what time the resident gets up?	(N = 44)	(N = 49)	(N = 45)	12.81^a	$.03^c$
Resident	18	57	53		
Staff	82	43	47		
Who decides when the resident takes a shower?	(N = 48)	(N = 48)	(N = 46)	21.13^a	$.32^c$
Resident	40	85	91		
Staff	60	15	9		
Who decides when the resident gets a haircut or has her hair done?	(N = 44)	(N = 46)	(N = 46)	5.89^b	$.17^c$
Resident	25	52	46		
Staff	75	48	54		

a $p < .001$, df = 1
b $p < .05$, df = 1
c not significant

Source: Data compiled by the authors.

use coin-operated machines and dryers, which were available outside of Gatewood at launderettes. In contrast to the practice at state schools, residents were expected to determine when their clothes needed washing, and had to bring their laundry to the area at Gatewood where the washing machine and dryer were located.

One reason why there is less concern with scheduling, orderliness, and neatness at Gatewood is that there is no less able population requiring continuous custodial care (such as toileting, feeding, bathing, and dressing). Residents are responsible for cleaning the entire facility, not just their own rooms. Yet the facility was easy to maintain and the staff spent little time supervising housekeeping details. However, the staff did consider cleaning a major activity for the residents; they spent most of the early morning hours supervising the cleaning and straightening up of rooms. Notes were left for residents who worked, specifying that they had to make their beds or help in cleaning the bathrooms. Women residents felt that cleaning was an important obligation for them and that it could be used, if desired, as an excuse for not coming to group counseling meetings.

Increased access to the community for work and leisure-time activities and interest in independent living has not been accompanied by the teaching of self-care skills necessary for community living. The educational program at the facility has focused on practical learning, such as recognition of coins of different values, but has not included training in skills in independent living such as eating in restaurants or marketing. Some interest and increased access to knowledge about food preparation is evident. Respondents were asked, "If you had to make breakfast for yourself, what would you do?" Answers were coded according to whether they were appropriate to the task at hand. While a majority answered appropriately during the first interview by saying "cook it" or "make it," during the second interview every respondent who answered this question gave such an answer (Table 8.2). After some seven to ten months of community living, respondents also appeared to interviewers to be much more confident that they could make breakfast for themselves. It should be noted that during the third interview there were slightly fewer respondents making this claim. While caution has to be exercised about respondents' claims made for skills possessed, as opposed to the examination of actual skills, at the very least respondents seem to recognize the importance of these skills as prerequisites for apartment living or any other independent living arrangement.

In order to determine the validity of claims made about being able to prepare one's own breakfast, respondents were asked to tell interviewers how they would prepare food. Significantly, more residents were able to provide detailed instructions on how to cook or

TABLE 8.2

Percent of Residents Able to Describe
How to Prepare Breakfast Appropriately
While Living at State School and Gatewood

Appropriateness of Description	Interview		
	I Upon Relocation (N = 47)	II After 7-10 Mos. (N = 42)	III After 16-20 Mos. (N = 45)
Appropriate	83	100	93
Inappropriate	17	0	7

Note: For interviews I and II X^2 = 5.91, p < .05, df = 1; for interviews II and III X^2 = 1.24 (not significant).
Source: Data compiled by the authors.

prepare a breakfast during the second interview than during the first (Table 8.3). This change occurred without a training program. However, the percentage of respondents who could provide highly detailed descriptions of preparing food dropped 18 percent from the second to the third interview. Even though only 15 percent of the respondents were able to describe in a detailed way the procedures learned earlier for making breakfast, there is no program at Gatewood for training residents how to cook. Some residents may have learned these skills by virtue of direct observation of kitchen tasks, since the kitchen was accessible to some residents. Others may have learned these skills when visiting their homes. It is possible that many other residents could learn how to cook if trained.

All activities in the state school were available within its confines, and there was little in the way of choice about where to go and what to do. A trend was evident during the first year at Gatewood for residents to become aware of a new organizational framework; their needs were to be partly provided for by institutions which were not part of Gatewood. Working at a sheltered workshop was considered as a way to earn money for breakfast; also YMCA's and settlement houses were thought of as places to pursue new interests such as photography. The new daily round of life was characterized by far greater decentralization of services and programs, with traveling on public transportation and other skills in urban living being highly

TABLE 8.3

Percent of Residents Able to Describe
Preparation of Breakfast at State School and Gatewood,
by Degree of Detail in Description

	Interview		
	I	II	III
	Upon	After	After
Degree of Detail in	Relocation	7-10 Mos.	16-20 Mos.
Description	(N = 43)	(N = 37)	(N = 42)
Highly detailed	14	32	14
Low detail	70	67	69
Only lists food items	16	0	17

Note: For interviews I and II X^2 = 9.05, p < .05, df = 2; for interviews II and III X^2 = 9.01, p < .05, df = 2.
Source: Data compiled by the authors.

important in order to be able to take advantage of the new activities. Accordingly, each resident would now not only have greater responsibility for making decisions about when to do things related to Gatewood, but would also have to initiate more activities in the community.

Greater independence on the part of residents results from a reduction of internal organizational constraints that prevent personal decision-making on their part (namely, the lack of a need for tight scheduling for large numbers of patients) and the limited services available at the residence, which produce as a result the need to utilize the community in order to meet all the needs of the residents. These two constraints, the relaxing of internal bureaucratic coordination and the external availability of experiences, are linked by the resident, who must adapt to a situation unlike that at the state school.

With the reduction of internal constraints, there is a kind of transfer of rights regarding personal life back to the mentally retarded person, from whom they were withdrawn while he was a patient at a state school. In this way it may enhance the self-image of the retarded person to be able to gain or regain some control over his personal life. Yet these personal decisions may only become meaningful when the resident has some larger purpose or central life interest. A minor decision as to what time one goes to bed requires a reason to make it important as a source of self-respect, and, for the former state school patient, having work provides that reason.

The necessity of utilizing community-based facilities for non-residential services may involve learning a new social structure and unlearning the social structure of the state school. The mentally retarded person who lived at a state school now must not only learn how to travel but also learn where he must go for certain activities and where he is not permitted to go at all. A new division of labor regarding services is present, and a new set of rules concerning where one may go and what one does in public is required.

SOCIAL SKILLS

It is reasonable to expect that new social skills would be required as a correlate of having to acquire services outside of the residential setting and having to deal with other residents as peers. Persons who were identified as patients at a state school were not ordinarily accustomed to providing information to others which would validate this ascribed role. Many familiar examples of how people provide information to others (which confirms their right to be present) are evident; dress and demeanor are the most available information used by others when they look us over. People may routinely arrive at the doors of an elevator, see someone standing there, and still compulsively push the button, even when it is already lit. This is one of the many small ways in which people establish their harmless intent to others in public places.

In any total institution, including state schools, the presence alone of patients constitutes their right to be present. Since they are in custodial care they need not do anything to prove their right to be there. By virtue of the purposes of these institutions, any behavior could be regarded as information which justified a person's presence, particularly bizarre actions. Alternatively, other actions which are perfectly appropriate for any situation may be ignored and the odd behavior be attended to, and regarded as part of the condition of mental retardation. Having to establish one's right to be present or explaining why one did something is not necessary for a patient at a state school. The role of patient, being ascribed rather than achieved, may be performed with little enthusiasm and little intent.

In contrast, a great array of social skills are necessary to establish one's behavior if one is asked to engage in an effort to correct mistakes when they are made. These skills are also part of living in a community residence such as Gatewood, where the staff assume that residents are able to account for their behavior and make some effort to correct their mistakes. Being responsible for behavior is something that the director of Gatewood was very concerned about. Often, after occurrences of conflict or violence he would ask residents why they had hit another person, and was amazed to find that they could not give an explanation for their behavior. Being able to give an explanation would also be a useful skill in public places when other people might assume that a retarded person who was present was able to read and tell time. Explaining a limitation might also make it possible for others to account for behavior they previously regarded as bizarre or suspicious.

HYPOTHETICAL SITUATIONS

It is of great interest in this study of relocation of mentally retarded adults to determine whether their social skills increase, decrease, or remain the same after they move. In order to examine social skills quite apart from such self-care skills as being able to travel or dress, a set of six questions was developed and asked during the three interviews. Each question provided residents with hypothetical dilemmas involving interaction with other people. Respondents were asked what they would do if faced with the social situation described in the hypothetical event. Questions involved potential responses whereby residents would have to initiate interaction, correct others, make needs known to others who were being annoying, retrieve property, or await an apology. In every instance, it was possible for the respondent to act in a cooperative way or act in a way which would promote conflict. As will be seen below, all situations were events which could be handled in several ways, depending on the response selected by the respondent. After each hypothetical situation was presented, respondents were asked, ''What would you do?''

1. Suppose an aide is holding your money and you want it but he is on the telephone.
2. Suppose a new resident moves in at Gatewood. You don't know him/her but you would like to meet him/her.
3. Suppose a resident is using your radio but he/she didn't ask if he/she could use it.
4. Suppose an aide steps on your toe accidentally.
5. Suppose your roommate plays his/her radio late at night and you cannot sleep.
6. Suppose the resident next door keeps everyone awake by playing his/her radio. By mistake, the aide punishes you by taking away your radio.

While it was anticipated that the new living arrangements at Gatewood would promote the acquisition of a new set of social skills appropriate for that facility, no statistically significant results were found in any of the questions, when distributions were compared from the first to the second interview and from the second to the third. This finding may result from the quality of the instrument used to examine the presence or absence of social skills, or from lack of verbal facility. The results also correspond with the impressions of the staff at Gatewood and the research team, which were that many residents lacked the array of skills for interaction with other people which would be appropriate for community living. It is possible that differences may emerge when comparisons are made with regard to answers to questions on social skills with a longer period of time between interviews.

In summary, there was some movement on the part of residents toward greater readiness for self-reliance and limited independence. In particular, personal decision-making was increased while living at Gatewood, while major decisions such as vocational rehabilitation placement were still being made by the staff. The skills taught to residents were mainly those which made up for unavailable programs and were predicated on current living arrangements. Skills involving such items of self-care as cooking, marketing, and eating in restaurants were not taught, since meals were prepared by the staff at Gatewood without extensive involvement by residents. Alternatively, vacuum cleaning and lawn mowing were taught because of the need for labor in these areas. Despite the use of the community for services, residents were trained only in those areas of living which could not be provided for by the staff. While movement out of Gatewood did occur, it was not based on extensive planning specifically designed to enhance each resident's adaptive and social skills in the community.

9

SOCIAL PARTICIPATION
IN THE LARGER
COMMUNITY

As was shown in Chapter Six, Gatewood provided new experience in cooperative living with others as well as opportunities to lead a normal-appearing round of life, based on the separation of home and workplace. Participation in vocational rehabilitation programs at sheltered workshops fulfilled a central and often explicitly expressed interest in being a worker who brought home a pay check. Work was also an important way to widen the social network of the residents. The workshop became a center of activity which provided a somewhat different social circle than the one available at the residence. Further, Gatewood residents met other peers at work who lived with their families. The result of this was the establishment of new friendships outside the Gatewood social circle. Of those residents who reported friendships with members of the opposite sex, the data gathered indicate that (1) friendships made at the state training school were dissolving; (2) new friendships were being established at Gatewood; and (3) there was a steady increase in the number of friendships formed at the workshop. However, the surrounding community has not been the source of many new friendships for Gatewood residents. Those friendships which developed in the workshop did not seem to extend beyond working hours. Of those who did report friendships with members of the opposite sex, one-quarter met their girlfriends or boyfriends at the workshop. This would seem to indicate that residents were aware of the social opportunities available in this setting and attempted to take advantage of them.

The workshop did not provide the sharp separation of workplace and home found in the lives of other community residents who work. For example, the companionship the Gatewood resident enjoyed in travel eased the transition from the place of residence to the place of work. As many as ten people from Gatewood were in training at one time at the same workshop and the experience of traveling

together to work may have also helped to maintain existing social relationships between those who were similarly situated. Further, Gatewood residents who attended the same training program often ate their
lunch together while at the workshop. In general, the workshop is a
place where purely sociable interaction among trainees takes place
during periods of free time such as coffee breaks. Almost three-
quarters of the sample ate lunch with another trainee or group of
trainees, and almost half spent their coffee breaks interacting with
other workshop trainees.

In the third interview, a number of questions were asked about
social participation in the larger community. When placement in
sheltered workshops was finally achieved, travel to work was either
independent or done in the company of a resident who could see to it
that other workshop trainees from Gatewood arrived and returned
safely. Occasionally residents were lost or separated on subways or
buses, but for the most part travel unaccompanied by staff members
was quite successful. Of those who had to travel to their workshop,
73 percent were able to give detailed accounts of how they traveled to
work, reporting bus or train numbers and stops. The responses suggested that those who could not give detailed accounts of their travel
were accompanied and aided by more able residents.

The separation of domicile, workplace, and recreation resulted
from staff reliance on the community for jobs and entertainment. This
dependence of the residents on the community, a seeming inconven-
ience for handicapped people, was in fact their preference. Two-thirds
of the residents expressed a desire to utilize their free time on weekends for activities which would take them away from Gatewood. Of
these respondents, half named places of entertainment generally available to all who lived in the community. The remainder preferred to
visit friends, relatives, or other specific locations they knew about.
Only a small minority did not report any specific location or activity,
or reported an unrealistic aspiration, such as foreign travel.

Local community centers and other facilities which were used
for sports and the pursuit of other interests such as crafts were
occasionally complemented by solo or paired expeditions to centers
of mass entertainment, such as movie theaters. Half of the respondents reported that they went to outside activities on their days off.
Of this subsample, one-third traveled to distant places for these activities, making independent use of public transportation. Competency
in using public transportation was further verified by the fact that
almost three-quarters of those who traveled were able to give detailed accounts of their route, including such information as bus or
train numbers, stops and streets.

Residents generally lived more adventurously and with greater
enthusiasm for seeing new things while living at Gatewood than while

living at the state school. Going off on their own or with a companion
to areas of the city where there is a great deal of cheap mass entertainment provided a potential outlet for their interests and for their
need to disidentify with being mentally retarded. This occurred more
often for male than female respondents.

USE OF THE COMMUNITY

Because Gatewood was designed to reintegrate mentally retarded
adults from state schools into the fabric of community life, it is important to examine the extent to which residents used the community,
through self-initiated activities or even through outings sponsored by
the Gatewood staff. In order to avoid characterizing Gatewood as
merely a "mini-institution" it is necessary to look for evidence of
the independent use of the community apart from sponsored group
activities. During the third interview, respondents were asked whether
they had engaged in any of thirteen activities or gone to establishments
outside of Gatewood since residing there. (For a list of these activities
see section III of the third interview, reproduced in Appendix B.) A
range of activities and establishments was chosen so as to include
some which lend themselves to mass activities, and others which were
more conducive to individuated activity. The items used are considered to represent some of the conventional types of behavior adults
might engage in while searching for diversions, companionship, or
entertainment. If respondents reported engaging in an activity, a
follow-up question was asked to determine whether they had attended
by themselves, were accompanied by some other non-staff person,
most likely a peer, or had been with a Gatewood staff member. In this
way we were able to determine the activity and with whom it was
shared.

Residents reported having gone to an average of 7.4 places out
of the 13 possible choices (see Table 9.1). The most frequently mentioned places were those within walking distance of Gatewood, namely,
the store, the park, and the church. These locations were also the
places that residents were first encouraged to use when relocated at
Gatewood, because of their close proximity to the residence. The
least frequently mentioned activities were those which involved individual activities dependent upon invitations from persons in the
community or upon being accompanied by fellow residents to social
regions where entry is more restricted than public parks or shopping
areas. For example, fewer than one-third of Gatewood residents
attended parties outside the residence.

TABLE 9.1

Percent of Gatewood Residents Attending
Outside Activities, and Form of Participation

Location or Activity Resident Named	Percent of Total Sample Reporting Participation (N = 48)	Of Those Who Reported Participation, Percent Who Participated:		
		Alone	With Other Non-staff Person	With Gatewood Staff Member
Store	94	78	16	7
Park	83	35	18	48
Church	75	31	28	42
Zoo	73	11	11	77
Movie theater	64	20	27	53
Parents	60	66	34	
Restaurant	58	21	32	46
Museum	54	4		96
Friends	48	48	39	13
Ball game	42	10	15	75
Community center	33	26	6	69
Party	31	13	47	40
Bar	23	64	36	
Other	16	29	14	57

Source: Data compiled by the authors.

While these data add to our overall knowledge of Gatewood residents' use of specific community facilities, we would like to consider
how these mentally retarded adults from state schools participated in
the larger community. From this problem a number of specific research questions can be derived. First, what is the relationship between the content of these activities and the social forms of participation? Second, do activities which require planning tend to involve
staff persons in a disproportionate number of instances? Finally, is
there a tendency for residents to engage in certain activities by themselves or with peers? One way of answering these questions is to
examine the characteristics of the residents' leisure time activities.
In so doing we have located a number of variable qualities which in
combination distinguish one activity from the other. For purposes of

analysis it is useful to discuss the activities in terms of five structural
dimensions, namely, distance, style of participation, frequency, time,
and the nature of the social region involved.

We also wanted to know whether an activity was close by, or
distant from Gatewood. Was it within easy walking distance or did it
require the use of transportation? We further wanted to know whether,
from the point of view of residents, an activity was part of the routine
round of leisure or was viewed as an "occasion." For example, entering a bar may be considered for normal persons a routine activity.
But for the residents of Gatewood we found it was an exceptional and
in fact an exotic experience. The important point is that it is not
merely formalized excursions that are exceptional; for Gatewood residents, any social interaction is exceptional in settings which are
out of the routine round of leisure time activity.

The style of participation in an activity denotes characteristics
of collectivism and individuation. Was participation parallel to or in
direct interaction with others? The principal criterion is not solely
the physical characteristics of the setting, but the social characteristics of the activity. While attending a movie involves physical pro-
pinquity to a large number of other theater patrons, it can be seen that
the norms of decorum in a movie theater mark out a highly individual
social region, within which the spectator views the performance.

The temporal aspects of leisure activity depend on the degree
to which an activity is scheduled or unscheduled. This dimension appears easier to arrive at than it actually is. The first criterion involves the degree of negotiation which may be available in establishing an appointment for participation. For example, meetings with
friends or parents may be scheduled to suit the convenience of both
the Gatewood resident and the other involved, taking into account other
obligations each person is required to meet. However, an invitation
to a party is not subject to negotiation. If the person invited cannot
come at a fixed time then he must arrive late or not at all. Typically,
parties are scheduled for the convenience of the greatest number, but
they are not subject to negotiation. This feature of the event is related to the second criterion, the degree to which the activity itself
operates on its own schedule. Ball games, museums, zoos, churches,
and community centers all function within their own relatively limited
operational timetable. On the other hand, store windows, parks, fast
food restaurants and similar places tend to be accessible either during highly extended hours of operation or have no fixed hours at all.

Finally, social regions may be either public or private. A region may be closed or open with regard to two points, namely who
is permitted to be present and how are those present expected to behave? First, is the establishment itself open to any person who meets
the entrance requirements? That is, if one goes to a fast food

restaurant one is normally expected to consume food. One doesn't go
there to quietly discuss business, or to engage in courtship or com-
radely banter. However, not all establishments open to the public operate on the basis of one large, public social region. Bars in particular,
because of the physical appointments such as booths and dim lighting,
encourage the establishment of private social regions within their confines. Likewise, community centers are private not only insofar as
use of them is limited to persons authorized either by membership or
place of residence, but also by the structure of small group activities
such as ping pong games and the like. Therefore, the second criterion
for allocating activities along this dimension is the degree of social
connection between the participant and the social region.

The thirteen activities asked about in the interview have been
classified, according to the five dichotomies mentioned above, to examine the relationship between these characteristics and their social
form. It is now possible to develop a profile of the activities engaged
in by our sample, according to whether they were done alone, with
non-staff persons, or with Gatewood staff. The total number of reported activities has been cross-tabulated against the mode of participation for each of the five dimensions. Table 9.2 reveals that when
Gatewood residents engage in an activity by themselves, it is most
often near the residence, routine in occurrence, individuated, private,
and not scheduled. When they are accompanied by staff, the profile
represents an organized excursion, one to a distant place, not part of
the daily routine, done as a collectivity, usually scheduled, and most
often ending in a place open to the public. Activities in which Gatewood
residents participate with a non-staff person present a more ambigu-
ous portrait. They are as likely to be at a distance as they are to be
close by the residence, and as likely to be routine as to be out of the
routine. However, they are activities which are individuated, take
place in private regions, and are not scheduled. They may, for example, be outings with other residents or with parents. It is possible
that Gatewood residents engage in activities with non-staff persons
not for the sake of seeing something new or exciting, but for the emotional satisfactions which come from the relationship with a relative
or peer. However, based on the available data this assertion cannot
be made with assurance. It is apparent that while Gatewood residents
self-reliantly frequent places in the immediate surrounding community, they are for the most part either less able or not sufficiently
encouraged to use the rest of the urban environment independently.

Our concern with the effectiveness of Gatewood in promoting
social participation in the wider community is not focused so much
on those who engage in activities by themselves as it is with what
seems to be a current pattern of dependence on staff. Residents attended an average of 2.5 activities by themselves, 1.6 activities

TABLE 9.2

Percent of Activities Attended Alone,
with Other Non-Staff Persons, and with Gatewood Staff,
by Type of Activity

| Type of Activity | Form of Participation | | | |
	Alone	With non-staff person	With staff	N =
Distant	22.5	21.6	53.0	194
Close	45.9	22.6	31.4	159
Routine	54.4	21.9	32.6	196
Exceptional	21.0	22.2	56.6	157
Collective	16.2	16.9	66.9	148
Individuated	47.9	25.9	26.3	205
Scheduled	16.9	18.5	64.6	178
Unscheduled	52.6	25.7	21.7	175
Public	30.4	18.5	51.1	260
Private	46.2	32.2	21.5	93

Source: Data compiled by the authors.

accompanied by non-staff persons, and 3.2 activities accompanied by
staff. Are these levels of participation according to different social
characteristics of outside activities significantly different from one
another? If they are significantly different, is it possible to make any
generalizations regarding the functioning of Gatewood and its residents?

Gatewood residents use the community in conjunction with their
peers substantially less often than they use it either on their own or
with staff. A comparison of the mean number of activities attended
alone to the mean number of activities attended accompanied by staff
reveals no significant differences either substantively or statistically
(see Table 9.3). As has been shown, the actual activity content of these
modes of participation are markedly different. However, the rate of
participation seems to be quite similar. A further comparison of the
mean number of activities attended with non-staff persons to the mean
number of activities attended alone does reveal statistically significant differences. Similarly, comparing the mean number of activities
with non-staff to the mean number of activities with Gatewood staff
also yields statistically significant results.

TABLE 9.3

Number of Activities Per Person Attended Alone,
Accompanied by Other Non-Staff Person,
and Accompanied by Staff Members,
and Total Number of Activities Per Person

| Number of Activities | Total Percent of Activities Attended (N = 48) | Percent Attended by Gatewood Resident | | |
		Alone (N = 48)	With Non-staff Person (N = 48)	With Staff Member (N = 48)
0	2	19	31	2
1-3	6	56	54	52
4-6	25	19	15	40
7-9	44	6	—	6
10 or more	23	—	—	—
Mean	7.4	2.5[a]	1.6[b]	3.2
Mode	7	2	1	4

[a] t between alone and staff not significant; t between alone and other non-staff persons p. = < .05

[b] t between other non-staff person and staff members p. = < .001

Source: Data compiled by the authors.

This current pattern of dependence upon the Gatewood staff for certain leisure time activities not only affected the way in which Gatewood residents used distant parts of the city but also influenced some types of social relations in the immediate environment. Gatewood residents rarely established informal social relationships outside of the social establishments (that is, the residence itself and workshops) in which they were regarded as participating members. Only one person mentioned having a girlfriend who was met outside of the workshop or the residence. Edgerton notes that former state school patients released into the community in California were able to establish protective relationships with those who lived near them (1967, pp. 192-204). The Gatewood residents provided little indication that such "benefactor" roles were being performed for them by those not affiliated with the residential facility and not part of the respondent's family. Only 10 percent of the respondents indicated that they received help from people they had met in the community since being resettled and it was not clear from the interviews as to precisely what was being provided in the form of help from these associates. Since most residents are in frequent contact with human service professionals both at the residence and at the workshop, the need for developing a protective relationship with a normal person living in the community may not be very strong among the Gatewood population.

At least within the two years of the study, Gatewood residents, within specified limits, used the community for the most part either with the aid of staff members or on their own. Moreover, the activities for which Gatewood residents were dependent upon staff were those which required planning, knowledge of time and place of activities, and the coordination of travel plans. Yet Edgerton and Dingman (1964) have demonstrated that moderately retarded persons, at least those having to make these decisions within an institution, can manage the problems of time and place in planning activities. Bjannes and Butler (1974) have noted differential patterns of restriction on the use of leisure time in bed and board facilities and family care situations, suggesting that the organizational constraints of the managed community may be responsible for the continued dependence upon the staff.

If we seek to identify instances of conventional behavior, the findings indicate a more varied situation. It is significant, for example, that some men from Gatewood use alcoholic beverages. Although only one-fifth of our sample went to a bar during the study period, it is a surprising finding that such a large proportion began to engage in behavior which, though conventional for normal persons, is nevertheless a social activity with which few of our sample had had much prior experience. Put even more strongly, drinking is an activity which traditionally was looked askance at for mentally subnormal persons. Engaging in an activity by oneself may be indicative of the greater privacy and autonomy these individuals have achieved. Conversely, to depend upon the Gatewood staff for direction in using the community may be indicative of the need for further evidence of adaptive skills before higher levels of independence and community integration are attained.

CITY LIFE AND GATEWOOD RESIDENTS

After many years of separation from city life, with all its attractions and dangers, Gatewood residents found much to engage them in their own environment. The subways were regarded as a place for adventure, even to the point that losing one's way on this complicated transit system was recounted with enthusiasm to other

residents and to staff. Gradually their new location in the city made
residents recognize that different behaviors were required for urban
living than were required for living at a state school. While becoming
more habituated to being among strangers, these retarded adults also
became more concerned with how they appeared to others in public
places.

Coming from a social environment which did not strongly differentiate between public and private places, these mentally retarded
adults had to learn how to establish their right to be present in public
places by demonstrating the appropriate behavior. In so doing, they
would become less noticed in public and more able to put others at
their ease outside Gatewood's confines. The social skills involved in
using streets for pedestrian activity, for example, involves more than
merely walking from one place to another; it involves providing cues
that one is willing and able to cooperate, that one is in control of one's
body, and that one is able to monitor the behavior of others as well as
one's own (Wolff 1973, p. 44). Many former state school patients had
not had to learn how to act as ordinary and competent pedestrians on
busy public streets because they did not use public streets while living
at state schools. Similarly, if they were with companions, they did not
learn how to keep in contact with them while walking and thus demonstrate to strangers that they and their companions constituted a social
unit.

Providing respect for others in public places was also something
that was not learned at state schools. A mentally retarded person in
a public place may stare a great deal at other people, constituting a
threat or challenge that others may take seriously. When retarded
adults cluster together in large numbers, this can be attention-getting
in itself, particularly if they are with a person who is "in charge of
them," which reinforces the idea that they cannot take care of themselves. Finally, in depending on a leader they may not learn the social
skills necessary for use of the streets.

A related matter which did draw some attention in public places
was the dress and appearance of the residents. When resettlement
first took place, the clothing selected for wear in public was often
outlandish by community standards. Gradually, through staff intervention and resident recognition of current styles, the dress of these
mentally retarded adults began to fit into the fashions of the people
who lived in the surrounding region. Moreover, men and women both
began to wear longer hair and the men started to sport moustaches
and beards.

During the two years when Gatewood was under study, we
learned from our interviews that the male residents were able to
use the streets and other public places in an unobstrusive manner,
to the extent that few incidents of conflict were reported in the com-

munity. Men would go off on their own with a companion to areas of
the city where there was a great deal of mass entertainment. On the
crowded boardwalks of seaside recreation areas or in the streets
around the downtown theater district, these men have found interesting
things to do. Retarded adults might find them attractive as special
regions for entertainment, but they are also locations where it is possible to blend into the crowd and not call attention to oneself. There
is little danger of retarded adults being excluded because they are
different in places where people are encouraged to walk about and
spend their money, moving from activity to activity without taking
too much notice of others. Moreover, the crowd itself is a form of
entertainment for people whose past movements were constrained by
institutional living arrangements.

Perhaps passing as just another person in the crowd may be an
important source of self-esteem for people stigmatized either because
they feel that people will avoid them because they are from a state
school, and because they know that they cannot meet the expectations
of others that they be verbally competent. Access to the districts of
the city where entertainment and amusement are located may provide
not only social occasions where mentally retarded adults can enhance
their self-image by feeling that they are part of something larger than
the residential community but may also help them to develop social
competence.

The metropolis provides much of the same lure for the Gatewood residents that it does for many other people. Robert E. Park
noted in his 1925 essay "The City" that urban living brings people
outside of themselves but also provides opportunities to find some
fulfillment. He writes:

> . . . in the long run every individual finds somewhere
> among the varied manifestations of city life the sort of
> environment in which he expands and feels at ease; finds
> in short, the moral climate in which his peculiar nature
> obtains the stimulations that bring his innate disposition
> to full and free expression. It is, I suspect, motives of
> this kind which have their basis, not in interests nor even
> in sentiment but in something more fundamental and prim-
> itive which draw away many, if not most, of the young
> men and women from the security of their homes in the
> country into the big, booming confusion and excitement
> of city life. In a small community it is the normal man,
> the man without eccentricity or genius who seems likely
> to succeed. The small community often tolerates eccen-
> tricity. The city, on the contrary, rewards it. Neither
> the criminal, the defective, nor the genius has the same

opportunity to develop his innate disposition in a small
town that he invariably finds in the great city. (Park 1967,
pp. 40-41)

Yet the mentally retarded are different, and this difference
makes them want to be like others whom they regard as unstigmatized.
People who are unstigmatized may be regarded as being in the equally
paradoxical situation of wanting to appear different from others in order to be accepted. Hence, the development of publics in urban life
provides an opportunity for competent people to feel part of an ex-
clusive experience, restricted to members of that social region. The
city provides a place for the mentally retarded adult to be somebody
by virtue of his new found normality, a characteristic need as much
a part of his being as his incompetence. Park's concept of the "moral
region" refers to closed social networks set apart from the other
moral regions of the city, where individual tastes and temperaments
are tolerated. The lure and attraction of a moral region is in its
openness for individual experience, as well as its exclusiveness. As
Park writes: "A moral region is not necessarily a place of abode.
It may be a mere rendezvous, a place of resort." (Park 1967, p. 43).
The data on social participation indicate that there are few
opportunities outside of residence and workshop for Gatewood residents to feel part of an ongoing social experience. As members of a
managed community their social experiences are limited to some extent by the social organization of Gatewood. The staff of Gatewood
do not encourage independent travel beyond the local community during non-work hours. While this effort is not a result of official policy,
the staff by discouraging this travel are better able to make their
routine tasks predictable. If residents stay out late at night or become lost on public streets or transportation, a substantial amount
of staff time must be allocated to locate and return them to the residence. Restricting travel contradicts the goals of resettlement and
produces certain similarities to living in state schools; residents
must inform the staff of their whereabouts during the non-work hours.
In conclusion, it can be seen that easy access to the larger
community has its benefits and disadvantages. One outcome is that
some residents have acquired aspirations for more independent living
arrangements and for competitive employment. Indeed, two residents
have already achieved these goals. Being a resident and trainee may
be stations for some on the way to greater independence and greater
access to life experiences and social circles more like those available
to other people living in the city. To explore this point more fully,
longitudinal studies of longer duration are required.

REFERENCES

Bjannes, A. T. and E. W. Butler
    1974   "Environmental Variation in Community Care Facilities
            for Mentally Retarded Persons." American Journal of
            Mental Deficiency 78: 429-39.

Edgerton, R. B.
    1967   The Cloak of Competence. Berkeley and Los Angeles:
            University of California Press.

Edgerton, R. B. and H. F. Dingman
    1964   "Good Reasons for Bad Supervision: 'Dating' in a Hos-
            pital for the Mentally Retarded." The Psychiatric
            Quarterly Supplement, Part 2. Utica, New York: State
            Hospital Press.

Park, Robert E.
    1967   "The City: Suggestions for the Investigation of Human
            Behavior in the Urban Environment," in Robert E. Park
            and Ernest W. Burgess, The City. Chicago: University
            of Chicago Press, pp. 1-46.

Wolff, M.
    1973   "Notes on the Behavior of Pedestrians," in Arnold
            Birenbaum and Edward Sagarin, eds., People in Places:
            The Sociology of the Familiar. New York: Praeger
            Publishers, pp. 35-48.

The establishment of Gatewood, a managed community, a place to live voluntarily, but one in which the criteria for membership are not under the control of the members, represents an innovation in community-based services for the mentally retarded. Residents who were once extremely dependent on the staff of state schools for guidance in daily life were after eighteen months at Gatewood more able to be self-reliant. Thus, the effort to turn patients into residents validates much of Goffman's analysis of life in total institutions (1961). As the social situation changed from a total institution to a managed community, so too did the behavior, attitudes and social relationships of our respondents change correspondingly.

As an innovation in community-based services for the mentally retarded, it is quite possible that Gatewood may undergo changes in its organization which could reduce or increase opportunities for the development of more self-reliant behavior and alter the informal atmosphere of this form of residential living. Under certain social constraints, particularly the absence of opportunities for placements in sheltered workshops, managed communities for mentally retarded adults could become very much like the large and impersonal state schools where staff-directed activity prevails and where residents may be located in the community but are not necessarily of that community. Furthermore, the history of the development of the large and isolated state schools represents a warning to planners, because such residential facilities were also intended to be more humane than earlier arrangements for care.

The planning of Gatewood and the story of what has happened to its residents is not only of interest to those concerned with the sociological analysis of facilities established for those who cannot fully take care of themselves; it also provides some practical information for planners of new forms of community care for the mentally

retarded. Living in a residence in the city could be accomplished by
simple transfers of people from one organized form of care to another.
The establishment and coordination of necessary services (particularly vocational rehabilitation) require intensive planning, and, moreover, depend on a careful assessment of the needs of the residents
and on the creation of a new model for the life style of mentally retarded adults.

The residents of Gatewood themselves provide some indication
of how complex a task it is to establish and coordinate services and
to create a new model of the mentally retarded adult in the community.
They not only approved of the new way to live but also wanted to acquire even more independence, indicating a need for the planning of
other kinds of living units. The new experiences of living at Gatewood
and learning to work in vocational rehabilitation programs in sheltered
workshops permitted more conventional activities and greater involvement in adult activities than their past situation did. Consequently,
the staff's expectations for appropriate social behavior at Gatewood
and at workshops for these former state school patients were greatly
heightened. Furthermore, much of the activity involved in residents
performing social control functions was completely new for people who
previously were under very close supervision. While Gatewood residents became more self-reliant and developed closer personal and
social relationships with their peers, they still remained dependent
on staff for many services they could probably have learned to perform
for themselves. Most evident of these is the general lack of skill in
traveling to distant locales. Though they learned to travel to workshops, it was evident that they did not have the capacity to perform
the logistics of determining when scheduled events take place, when
to leave for them, and how to get there. In travel they maintained
their dependence on the Gatewood staff for direction and accompani-
ment to these places. Moreover, training is required to increase social and cognitive skills in the area of participation in the wider community, and in getting along at the residence as well. Before such a
program can be initiated, it must be determined whether it is within
the scope of the managed community to provide such a service.

EXPANDING THE CONCEPT OF NORMALIZATION

The experience of Gatewood sheds some light on normalization,
one of the concepts used to guide the establishment of community care
services for the mentally retarded. Using Scandinavian social welfare
policies as a model, some planners have attempted to apply normalization to the establishment of services in the United States

(Wolfensberger 1972). Their aim is to create programs which are coordinated but not centralized, ". . . making available to the mentally
retarded patterns and conditions of everyday life which are as close
as possible to the norms and patterns of the mainstream of society"
(Nirje 1969, p. 181).

Implicit in this concept is a sociological generalization, namely,
that the social surroundings in which people live will deeply influence
their opportunities to lead conventional lives. In addition, the social
environment is subject to judgment by others, not only as to who lives
there, but as to how they are to be treated and what can be expected
from them during their lives. Those who live in institutions are often
regarded as not having potential for growth and development. Normalization involves an approach that takes growth and development
into account as needs of mentally retarded people, and an understanding that mentally retarded people change during their life cycle, not
because their impairment is substantially altered, but because of the
unimpaired self which remains. Indeed, the principle of normalization
insists that the retarded person be defined as having a life cycle and
personal career independent of his socially defined status as inmate,
patient, and resident (Nirje 1969, pp. 181-83).

Two related questions are raised explicitly by this concept,
which guides program development: (1) What do people who cannot
take care of themselves have in common with other human beings?
(2) Under what social conditions are these common human characteristics fostered and sustained, and other, less desired characteristics modified or made less obtrusive?

Clearly, any new service model is built on a revised concept of
the impairment known as mental retardation, one which attributes far
more developmental capacity and need for self-regard than do earlier,
more one-dimensional models. The new model of the impairment
takes into account the additional handicap produced by the social environments designed to care for the mentally retarded. An additional
component of the new model is that it sees the impairment in more
complex ways, focusing on adaptive self-care and social skills as
well as on test scores.

The planners of services for the mentally retarded are concerned with the ways in which programs that, among other things,
separate mentally retarded persons from society, interfere with
the conventional rhythms of daily living and with the establishment
of ordinary social relationships and rewarding experiences for retarded people. Therefore, they pattern services to enhance community involvement, beyond focusing simply on the level of impairment
in the population served.

Furthermore, most mentally retarded adults are treated differently from children. In program construction, age-appropriate activi-

ties are considered necessary if mentally retarded people are to acquire self-regard. The programs consider that learning how to cope with the unprepared and unstructured situations of daily living is as important as fitting into the routine and regular rounds of life (Nirje 1969, p. 182). Therefore, it is thought that mentally retarded persons need to develop social skills and be familiar with situations in which others may not be aware of their limitations or alternatively, may be all too aware and may act in either a rejecting or patronizing way.

Despite recognition of the need to train mentally retarded people for unstructured situations, the principle of normalization needs much more explicit concern with the behavior of persons as strangers who come into the presence of others, and provide evidence to others of their meeting prior expectations or of being discrepant with them. The principle of normalization needs to become conceptually complete by dealing with the often unnoticed norms of social interaction found in urban society. Consequently we recommend a socially adaptive model of the self, based upon the way persons, as actors who come into contact with others, give off expressions to others as well as receiving expressions and taking in what others provide them. The model of the mentally retarded person requires an added element, a conception of the person-as-actor, one who is both influenced by others and, while he is present, influences others who may or may not know much about him. Normalization is the result of human activity; it is the act or process of making normal, and it involves active work on the part of all concerned to realize it.

How people make things "normal" is the subject of a long and fascinating essay by Erving Goffman in his recent book, Relations in Public (1972, pp. 238-333). Goffman, who has written about the management of stigma, is dealing now with normalization as it occurs among the ordinary and nonstigmatized in society. Like the stigmatized, the nonstigmatized have to control or at least be aware of the expressions they give off. For when contact is made with a stranger, others have to check him out ". . . to find him someone unalarming whom they can disattend in order to be free to get on with other matters" (Goffman 1972, p. 279).

Understandably, the person who does this all the time can be quite good at maintaining "normal appearances." In contrast, the person who has lived away from strangers and returns to the community may be alarming to others. The former state school patient may be unsure of his right to be present on certain occasions and may make other people present uncertain of what to expect from him. An escalating chain of error in understanding the intentions of the retarded person may begin, and an explanation may not be proffered by the former state school patient, who is used to being around others who know why he is there and do not question his right to be present.

In public places outside of "total institutions" (Goffman 1961), the information which one must produce in order to establish one's harmlessness to others, or one's right to be present is much more predicated on using the standard signs of innocuous disattention than it is within institutional boundaries. One way that this is done is by being "with" other people in groupings which do not draw attention to themselves by virtue of their size, or by the presence of a leader. Accordingly, if one does alarm others in some way, one must be aware of having this effect and must make an effort to explain the action which might appear strange. All these efforts to put others at their ease in contact among strangers involve the creation of "normal appearances." Reflexiveness in social interaction means treating your own actions as others would see them, or "taking the role of the other."

Such a sociological approach to the structuring of the self would broaden the principle of normalization to include the social skills needed to get through the day and to get others to validate one's claim to membership. This also means getting others to regard you as having the right to be present upon certain occasions, despite one's differentness. The former state school patient, as well as the mentally retarded person who was not "put away," has to learn how to recognize a social relationship that he has entered into, to recognize what it means for others as well as for himself, and to know the subtle gestures and words that are used by members of the community to reaffirm it. In addition, normalization involves not just being in unstructured situations, but also subjecting one's own actions to examination, an important way of getting others to regard you as a member of the community. Finally, normalization is contingent upon being able to account for what one can or cannot do, an unnecessary skill for persons in institutions where behavior, particularly bizarre behavior or lack of skills, only confirms the need for the person to be confined, his need for supervision and the hopelessness of any possibility of programs affecting his development as a person.

An interactionist approach should not conflict with the structural approach adopted by the proponents of normalization. It only points out areas of living which have great need for serious programming. Years of living in state schools can make people less aware of the expressions they give off. Members of the staff of state schools can easily disattend to the signs of developmental needs and aspirations of the patients because they expect the patients to overwhelmingly give off signs of aberration. Thus, the "normal appearances" of unaccountable behavior may be an adaptation to the routine certainties of state schools. Normalization, if it is to become a more adequate concept of services, must address itself not only to new routines, approximating the conventions and rhythms of everyday life in modern society, but also to socially adaptive skills which actors, even those considered mentally retarded, must possess to help in the activity of making things appear normal.

THE NEED FOR RESOCIALIZATION PROGRAMS

At Gatewood, some residents had a difficult time adjusting to their new social environment, particularly during the first six months when six residents went back to state schools. The mentally retarded adults who leaves a state school must be prepared after moving for the new social situations with which he will be faced once relocated in the managed community. Not only must he be told that he will go to live in the community and learn how to work, but he must learn the range of behaviors that are expected in the new residence and in public places. There is a need for a period of intensive training in situations which approximate those found in the new social situation. The establishment of such a program may increase the initial costs of resettlement, but may have long-run advantages in preventing transfers back to state schools.

Simply assigning staff at state schools to the task of resocialization or even of approximating expected patterns of living may not provide enough knowledge, ability, or the appropriate structured situation for such a period of intensive learning. The staff of the community residence itself has to be trained in the concept of the managed community and must have experience in working in such settings. It may be preferable to bring in staff from outside the state school to accomplish this important task. The content of these programs should include knowledge about how to get along with roommates, since roommates have a social relationship rarely found in state schools; it should include learning how to present oneself in public places in an unobtrusive manner or, alternatively, learning how to ask for help when it is needed, rather than merely standing around and waiting until it arrives; learning how to deal with interpersonal conflict without involving staff or using physical force; and unlearning the obsequious behavior which was brought along from state schools. There is a need for further study of the skills required for living at a community residence and how to teach them.

DIRECTIONS FOR FURTHER RESEARCH

Since one of the goals of this sociological analysis was to be able to predict the conditions under which resettlement would be successfully accomplished, an examination of the social characteristics of the resident population was completed. In the course of our analysis of the outcomes of resettlement, an effort was made to control for the following variables: (1) sex; (2) ethnicity; (3) intelligence as measured by I.Q. tests; (4) length of residence at the state school; (5) age at which the resident went to live at the state school; (6) family contact during the period of institutionalization; and (7) whether the resident was identified as having behavioral problems in the year previous to transfer to Gatewood.

Although some differences were noted, this analysis was unable to demonstrate any statistically significant and consistent association between the background characteristics of Gatewood residents and their social functioning once resettled. It must be emphasized that the lack of such relationships in this study does not mean that future investigations ought to dismiss them from consideration or that planners of other managed communities should not consider them as a possibility. The lack of association between background and outcome may be an artifact of this particular case study and/or an artifact of case studies as a method of investigation. First, the size of the sample itself is not large enough to allow for effective statistical controls on background characteristics, and it is possible that a larger sample with essentially the same range of characteristics might produce statistically significant differences. Second, the characteristics of the sample selection process were based on a planned procedure which may have produced a relatively homogeneous population for resettlement. As was shown in the Introduction, these procedures promoted uniformity in abilities and screened out people with behavior problems that consistently brought them to the attention of the authorities at state schools.

A larger sample could produce greater variation in the background of those resettled, enabling investigators to determine which characteristics are contributing factors to successful resettlement. Similarly, the relatively small size of managed communities of this type makes it difficult to generate a sufficiently large sample from any single residence. As a future strategy for investigators, we suggest a comparative approach in which a group of similar residences with matching organizational characteristics is studied. It would then be possible to correlate background with outcome and at the same time control for differences in social environment, if it was felt that there was variation from one managed community to another. The larger sample of cases generated from this procedure would provide a more adequate range of data from which to decide what background characteristics are conducive to successful adaptation to community living outside large and isolated state schools. It is not possible to draw any conclusions at this time about who adapts well to the managed community.

The movement from the state school to the community residence also raises questions about the consequences of different procedures of transferring people. Residents who were moved as a group from state schools seem to depend on each other for social support and constitute a peer group, while those who are relocated alone have a much sharper break with past associations and are forced to form new peer groups, break into existing closed groups, or remain socially isolated.

The rate of movement also may have an impact upon whether planners perceive the need for staff training. When a facility is filled slowly, residents may not be regarded by planners as requiring a program to orient them to the facility and the community. Similarly, staff skills may be regarded as unimportant because of the high ratio of staff to residents, making the need for a training program less visible to planners.

A number of other research issues are raised by this case study which are related to the background characteristics of residents and their potential for adaptation to community living, particularly for medium- or minimum-care residential facilities. The trend toward diversification in providing services for the mentally retarded in the community raises many questions about the appropriateness of certain kinds of residential units for intellectually homogeneous as compared with heterogeneous populations. These questions were rarely raised when Gatewood residents were originally selected for relocation from state schools because of the pressure to comply with court orders to reduce the populations at these large and isolated institutions. While it would not have been necessary for most of the Gatewood residents to live at state schools if adequate community services had been available at the time of placement, not every community residential facility is appropriate for every mentally retarded adult. Some facilities may be too demanding for severely retarded people, and the mildly retarded may feel that they could live more independently.

There seems to be no relationship between I.Q. and success in return to community living, at least insofar as success can be defined by managing to stay out of trouble in the community or at the residential facility. Mildly retarded persons are often found to have difficulties in getting along with staff members at community residential facilities and often act "bossy" with less able residents. Furthermore, they are more physically mobile in the community outside of the residence and more likely to get into trouble with neighbors and the police than are moderately retarded persons. Such persons may be in need of supportive services in the form of individual or group counseling, while more severely retarded persons may not require, or benefit from, such efforts.

Mildly retarded persons may not wish to be in a facility with other mentally retarded people and may thrive in a smaller residential setting, such as family care, which does not call attention to their disabilities or where they would not be in close informal social contact with the more profoundly mentally retarded. In the larger state school, mildly retarded persons often were used in service shops as helpers or were informally employed in the "back wards" to take care of what are called by these persons as "low grades" or "vegetables." A community residence provides fewer opportunities for mildly retarded persons to clearly demonstrate their competency and to differentiate themselves from those who are less able, through roles as helpers or work in service shops. Some residents have taken to not mentioning the fact that they were once in state schools and will refer euphemistically to their former location as "upstate."

The length of time spent at a state school may have an important impact on the extent to which resettlement in the community is possible. The person who has spent many years at a state school may initially find it difficult to be in an open-ended situation where he cannot always explain himself to strangers. While persons who spent long periods of time in state schools had some difficulty in learning to consciously use the appropriate cues while in public places, they also had to learn how to get along with each other when there was a greater necessity to be responsible for personal decision-making than before. Residents at Gatewood now in control of their direct allowance of $17.00 per month for personal expenses had to decide how to spend their money. At the state school, they had had an account at the store on the grounds. Since residents at Gatewood had to share a room with one other person, they now had to decide who would do what to maintain the room, rather than being told by attendants, as they were at the state schools, to do different tasks in the wards. Sharing was something that was not encouraged in state schools, where these persons lived in dormitories with other people. The kinds of social relationships between residents which are possible under differing social and physical conditions may influence the extent to which self-reliant behavior in the community and at the residence is encouraged or discouraged. Similarly, the relationship established between the resident and members of the staff may take on a different character under differing conditions. If staff spend less of their time directing and supervising residents in basic tasks of daily living (such as cleaning rooms), then they may become more available to residents for counseling them in the more complicated aspects of living in an urban community. The counseling role may be maximized when authority roles or punitive roles are downplayed or are differentiated.

A managed community may be conceived of as a microsocial environment within a larger social context. Many times the points of contact with the larger social environment encourage the development of self-reliance and appropriate behavior on the part of residents. When a facility is in close proximity to neighbors, staff become genuinely concerned about the appearance and mannerisms of residents. When a resident attends a vocational rehabilitation program in the community, he may become more self-regulating, knowing that if he does not get up at seven in the morning he will be late for work.

The resettlement of some mentally retarded adults at one community residence can only provide a way of raising questions about the extent to which mentally retarded adults in general can be reintegrated in the community. It is important to initiate and complete comparative sociological research on the subject of resettlement, organized around the following questions: (1) What kinds of social skills are needed to live in different residential settings? (2) Which socially learned and utilized skills acquired at state schools are appropriate and which inappropriate for community living?

A number of structural characteristics of residential care programs can be suggested as influencing the composition of the social environment of mentally retarded adults. These programs vary by (1) size; (2) availability of supportive human service networks; (3) availability of future placements in more independent settings; (4) availability of candidates for open places; (5) the extent to which the facility is integrated into the community; (6) the extent of coordination with vocational and recreational services; (7) the homogeneity of the population of the facility; (8) the extent to which residents have contact with family, friends, and neighbors in the community; (9) the degree of specialization of the facility; (10) staff training and staff-resident ratios; and (11) administrative goals and means of implementation.

The issues examined in the present study arose because of the existence of large and isolated institutions for the mentally retarded, and because it has become public policy that residential facilities should be changed so as to be near the families and homes of those who are retarded and to be closely coordinated with community services. While this issue is presently the focus of great public concern and interest, the current problem of the resettlement of mentally retarded people from state schools has deflected attention from the related social policy issue of providing supporting services, including residential care where needed, for the mentally retarded living with their families. The adaptation to residential care of mentally retarded who have been living with their families requires careful study, and may differ in many respects from the adaptation of mentally retarded persons moving away from long-term stays in large and

isolated institutions. Finally, it can be anticipated that public policy
and planning will lead to an increased flow of mentally retarded adults
from the community into facilities like Gatewood, reversing the current trend of filling community-based residential facilities mainly
with former state school patients.

In conclusion, there is a need to develop an understanding of the
network of services that are required by the returning state school
patients (and other mentally retarded adults), while carefully avoiding
the dangers of overprogramming, which can lead to a situation in
which mentally retarded adults never learn to act in a self-reliant
way. Such a network of services would have to include a variety of
clients and be able to fit them into different residential situations.
Future research on resettlement could identify the characteristics of
mentally retarded persons who are resettled from state schools, and
make precise determinations of the relationship between these characteristics and success in community living.

One of the practical uses of sociological investigation is to suggest, from the analysis of existing institutions, what is possible. The
managed community for the mentally retarded we called Gatewood
was seen by most of its residents as both a haven from the isolation
and inactivity of the state school and as a step in the direction of more
independence and participation in the wider community. In many ways
we share that vision of Gatewood with its residents, and agree that the
managed community is only a way station in living.

The mentally retarded adults who came to live at Gatewood were
not the first to leave state schools, but are among the first to participate in an elaborate program innovation in community-based relocation. Rather than consider them victims of outdated social policies,
it is far better to see them as consultants in an effort to create a network of services in the community for those who are not fully able to
take care of themselves. Community care of the retarded is possible,
and can be made more effective than it was during the time when Gatewood residents were under study. The emphasis on small residential
facilities in the community should not be regarded as a panacea; the
mentally retarded person requires a network of decentralized services to provide for his special needs, as well as for the needs he has
in common with normal people. An end to the large and overcrowded
state school must be seen as only the beginning of the implementation
of new concepts in community services for those who cannot fully take
care of themselves.

REFERENCES

Goffman, Erving
    1961   Asylums: Essays on the Social Situations of Mental Pa-
            tients and Other Inmates. New York: Anchor Books.

1972   Relations in Public: Microstudies of the Public Order.
        New York: Basic Books.
Nirje, Bengt
    1969   "The Normalization Principle and Its Human Manage-
            ment Implications," in Robert B. Kugel and Wolf
            Wolfensberger, eds., Changing Patterns of Residential
            Services for the Mentally Retarded. Washington, D.C.:
            Department of Health, Education, and Welfare, pp. 179-96.
Wolfensberger, Wolf
    1972   The Principle of Normalization in Human Services.
            Toronto: National Institute on Mental Retardation.

INTERVIEWING MENTALLY RETARDED ADULTS

Although there is an extensive literature on the techniques of interviewing (Hyman 1954, Richardson et al. 1965) there has been no consideration of the special problems involved in asking questions of mentally subnormal citizens either in the community or in custodial care. Recent efforts at data-gathering in psychiatric hospitals by Weinstein (1974) and Mayer (1974) indicate that interviewing is possible, but their research reports do not indicate that any special problems emerged for interviewers.

While the life situations of mentally retarded children and their families have been studied through the use of surveys (Saenger 1960) and structured open-ended interviews (Farber 1959, Birenbaum 1971), the mentally retarded have rarely been allowed to speak for themselves, even when they have the capacity to respond to questions. What kinds of special interviewing problems emerge when mentally retarded adults are asked to describe and evaluate their past and present experiences? What kinds of constraints are placed on the interview situation by the presence of a respondent who is identified as mentally retarded?

Erving Goffman notes in his discussion of the organization of experience by actors in everyday life that the mere presence of an actor in any situation who does not permit others to validate his competency will affect that social situation in a "diffusely relevant" way:

The properties we attributed to normal actors such as correct perception, personal will, a range of adult competencies, access to memory, a measure of empathy regarding others present, honesty, reliability, fixed social and personal identity, and the like are counted on in a multitude of ways whenever interpersonal dealings occur.

It follows that any apparent need to redefine an actor as possessing other than these conventional attributes can have a very pervasive effect upon the activity in which the altered person participates (1974, p. 188).

118

INTERVIEWERS

In the study reported on in this book, the interviews were conducted by the senior investigator, a male sociologist, and a female
psychologist who functioned primarily as an interviewer; men were
interviewed by a male interviewer and women by a female interviewer.* Interviews generally lasted between one-half hour and three-
quarters of an hour and were usually conducted in a room in which
no other people were present. One person out of the sample of 64
refused to complete an initial interview and was not reinterviewed.

Both interviewers had had a great deal of prior face-to-face
contact with mentally retarded adults, as well as extensive experience
in interviewing. By virtue of this combination of qualifications, no
special period of training was undertaken to familiarize them with
the effects on behavior of mental retardation or institutional life. The
tape recording of all interviews reaffirmed our decision to provide
no special training, since both interviewers were able to establish
rapport with respondents.

Prior to the third and final wave of interviews it was necessary
to bring the female interviewer who was not in continuous contact with
the project up to date on the progress of the study. In this briefing,
the female interviewer was informed about new issues which might
influence the course of the interviews, and might also allow her to
become familiar with additional questions and other modifications
resulting from these new concerns. Finally, it is worth noting that
the same interviewers interviewed the same respondents throughout
the three years of the study.

OTHER RESEARCH EXPERIENCE

The ethnographic research of Robert Edgerton provides a useful model related to both the examination of the everyday life experience of mentally retarded adults and the problem of gaining access

---

*Colombotos, Elinson, and Lowenstein (1973) suggest that there
is no difference in responses reported to male and female interviewers in a community survey collecting data on psychiatric symptoms.
Although they note the tentative nature of their findings, our impression is that the decision to match respondents and interviewers on
sex was a correct one.

to respondents. In both Edgerton's work and our own, the investigation was affiliated with mental retardation agencies, which presented the immediate problem of not representing the data-gathering process as a threat to potential respondents. The sample studied by Edgerton in Cloak of Competence (1967) was no longer living in an institutional setting and its members were particularly fearful of being reinstitutionalized. In addition, they were extremely fearful of being stigmatized as people from institutions. Finally, the mean I.Q. for this sample was 64, compared with 51 for our sample, making them, perhaps, more aware of the consequences of what they said and did.

Edgerton's strategy of gaining access to respondents was one of working toward a formal interview through protracted and highly informal contact. Interviewers were able to establish themselves as sympathetic figures in the often lonely lives of these mentally retarded adults. Then, "the interviewers were instructed to lead the respondent into a discussion of certain areas of interest by nondirectional questioning" (1967, p. 16). The result was that interviews were regarded as friendly and informal as well as being highly informative. As a result of this strategy, there were no refusals to cooperate and ". . . virtually no resistance or reticence . . ." (1967, p. 17).

In our study of the resettlement of retarded adults in a community residence, we were also faced with the problem of being identified as authority figures, but with a difference. First, both the interviewers had been known to respondents as part of the team of mental health workers who screened potential candidates for the community residence while the respondents were still patients at state schools. These visits to institutions, as well as frequent informal contact during participant observations at the residence during the interregnum between the first and second wave of interviews, established the senior investigator as an official, albeit benign, figure in the lives of the respondents. Some 65 hours of participant observation also made possible the acquisition of important observations on the respondents' face-to-face interaction with staff and other residents.

PROBLEMS OF INTERVIEWING

Two categories of problems are involved in interviewing retarded populations. The first group of problems derives from the interviewer's role and the interview situation. The second group of problems derives from the characteristics of the population being studied. It includes accessibility, cognitive problems, and respondent motivation.

The Role of the Interviewer

While contact with respondents had occurred over a considerable period of time before the first interview and between interviews, interviewers were not perceived as part of the staff of the residence or as people who had some influence over the lives of the respondents. The problem for the interviewer became one of maintaining this separate and distinct identity, despite the usefulness of being identified as an authority in order to gain cooperation for interviewing. Interviewers were seen as authorities from some outside supervisory agency, as people to complain to but not people who could punish residents for misbehavior.

Against the background of a population whose life experiences ranged from three to thirty-eight years of living in a state school, such a definition of our role, and its acceptance, were surprising. By virtue of the physical isolation of state schools, outside visits from friends and relatives were at best irregular, and contacts with strangers were few and far between. Consequently, respondents were used to interacting with either peers or state school staff, including physicians who were in charge of the wards or dormitories where they lived. As with other total institutions, those inmates who came to the attention of the authorities were those who violated the rules. Often a medical interview or a psychological testing situation was initiated by some patient's transgression and was followed by negative consequences, such as transfer to a more restricted and less desirable ward.

The design of the study itself promoted the gradual development of trust of the interviewer by respondents. Even though many of the same questions were repeated on successive interviews, no negative consequences ensued after the interview took place. Moreover, interviews were conducted by the same interviewers on all three occasions. Interviewers were regarded nonetheless as capable of effecting change in the lives of residents, and occasionally were asked for help in the solution of personal problems, either during the course of the interview or at other times. Significantly, contact with interviewers did not have the same "looping effect" that Goffman reports occurred in all total institutions he studied (1961, p. 37). When inmates confided in the staff in psychiatric hospitals, such information was used by other members of the staff to determine what action should be taken with patients.

While the interviewers were not perceived as authority figures who could punish, many direct requests for opportunities to work or for the acquisition of services were made, producing the expectation

on the part of the respondent that some outcome would be effected by
the intervention of the interviewer. Interviewers were required to
help the respondent develop an accurate definition of the situation
without creating an outright denial of the request. The interviewers
could not guarantee such things as placement in vocational rehabilitation programs, yet the outright denial of such requests could damage
the relationship of trust between the informant and the research staff.
Similarly, the interviewer could not become a consumer advocate for
respondents or an ombudsman without interfering with ongoing relationships established between respondents and staff of the residence
and between the interviewers and the staff. From the point of view of
what was best for the respondents, their ability to make their needs
known to staff, and the hope of an increase in their self-reliant behavior, it was important not to become direct spokespeople for residents. The interviewers handled this dilemma by indicating to the
respondent the appropriate person at the facility who could help in
solving his problem.

Accessibility

Information may be withheld inadvertently, or deliberately by
forgetfulness, by repressing painful or embarrassing situations, or
by simply not being able to control the content or extent of an answer.
Most respondents interviewed had difficulty in remembering details
of activities they claimed to have engaged in over the weekend previous to the interview, although they were able to describe their experience in broad terms. Among the types of information we were
most interested in collecting were data on whether our sample had
developed more conventional relationships with members of the opposite sex. Prior experience in cross-sex social relationships at
state schools had been limited to sponsored activities such as dances,
or covert trysts in wooded areas or unused buildings. Questions concerning cross-sex contact elicited extreme responses. Either too
much information was supplied, often with much irrelevant detail, or
there was too little information, given in the form of highly guarded
responses.

Cognitive Conditions

In order for a successful interview to take place, both interviewer and respondent must fully understand what is expected of each
other. As Charles Cannell and Robert Kahn note:

The respondent needs to know what constitutes successful
completion of his task; he needs to know the concepts and
frames of reference implied by the question, because they
define the criteria of response adequacy (1968, p. 543).

The interviewer can issue simple directions to the mentally retarded respondent as well as inform him of the purposes of the research and how he can help by taking part in an interview. However,
the questions themselves must also be broken down into small units,
using very few words. Even a fairly simple question has to be broken
down conceptually in order to encourage the respondent to answer, as
well as to make him feel that he can answer the question.

Words which have one meaning and usage for the interviewer
as a member of the larger society may have very different meanings
for respondents, often meanings shared only by mentally retarded persons from institutions. Some of these were discovered during the field
work conducted by the senior investigator at the state schools and this
information was passed on to the other interviewer during discussion
of the interview schedule.

Occasionally, respondents had developed quite private meanings
for words used during the interview, creating a situation of greater
uncertainty for the interviewers. These meanings may be discovered
at the stage in which the content of the interview is analyzed. However,
the usage of words with private meanings presents a more immediate
problem that affects the structure of the interview situation. In order
for the interviewer to intelligently probe for clarification of an am-
biguous response, he must be able to accurately interpret the previous statement. If a statement is inaccurately understood, a chain
of error may be initiated in which unnecessary probing will ensue.
Since the mentally retarded respondent provides very little nonverbal
feedback to the interviewer, the interviewer may continue to probe
when he clearly is leading the respondent down a path that will produce little in the way of useful information. Furthermore, the mentally retarded person may become increasingly frustrated by this
persistence in probing and may completely lose any connection between the probe and the originating question. When this occurred, we
proceeded to the next question.

Motivation

Motivation was sometimes problematic in interviewing mentally
retarded adults because of the social and political context in which

this research was conducted. Patients from state schools who were
resettled in the community residence had been the subject of investigative reporting by television networks and journalists. The inade-
quacy of these state-run facilities had come under intense political
and legal scrutinizing during the past few years and understandably
some respondents perceived the research effort as part of this re-
formist activity. Consequently, interviewers were seen as possible
allies in the efforts of residents to acquire better treatment, and residents were willing to share horror stories about conditions at state
institutions.

More conventional sources of motivation to cooperate with interviewers were only present to a limited degree in the interview situation, predominantly taking the form of wanting to help others as well
as be helped. Other investigators of interviewing have also emphasized the sociability dimension of the situation for the respondent as
well as the emotional satisfaction derived from having someone interested in one's story. As will be found in other interviews with people
from total institutions, there is a need to tell a "sad" tale as well as
a need for social stimulation (Goffman 1961, p. 151). Because of the
mentally retarded persons' problems in the areas of cognition, there
was no evidence in the interviews that intellectual satisfaction was
acquired from being a respondent.

Since many of our sample had been institutionalized for long
periods of time and had had few visitors (some had virtually none), the
interview situation provided what may be characterized as a surrogate
visit for the respondent. In this sense, the interview was as much a
part of the process of relocation as were the physical changes involved
in resettlement in the community. It can be said that respondent motivation depended quite strongly on the qualitative nature of the emotions
evoked by the interview process. With the mentally retarded adult becoming more and more involved in activities outside the residence,
they were not only more difficult to locate for interviews but were also
less enthusiastic about being interviewed.

CONCLUSIONS

The experience gained in the course of this study suggests that:
1. The interviewer is caught between two opposing pressures,
namely, the desire to establish rapport with respondents, and the
equally important goal of not being cast into the role of a benefactor,
either of the official or the unofficial variety.
2. An interviewer must always be aware that mentally retarded
respondents can provide much irrelevant information, and he must be

able to halt these trends before the point at which little useful information is elicited. Alternatively, if too little information is provided or if questions are not understood, the interviewer must be able to devise suitable probes, fitting into the general framework of subdividing questions into component parts.

3. Interviewers should be selected from personnel who either have prior experience in working with mentally retarded people or who are trained to engage in relaxed interaction with the mentally retarded. Interviewing the mentally retarded often involves disattending to behaviors which may seem bizarre to the uninitiated. This problem in the selection of interviewers introduces considerations of cost and time in training, a matter of no small moment in survey research.

The overall lesson to be learned is that prior reluctance to ask questions of this group and others similarly situated is based on the assumption that they are different from normal populations. Perhaps the question can be better put in positive form: how similar are these populations to normal people?

REFERENCES

Birenbaum, A.
  1971   "The Mentally Retarded Child in the Home and the
          Family Cycle." Journal of Health and Social Behavior
          12: 56-65.
Cannell, Charles F. and Robert L. Kahn
  1968   "Interviewing," in The Handbook of Social Psychology,
          second edition. Reading, Massachusetts: Addison-
          Wesley.
Colombotos, J., J. Elinson, and R. Loewenstein
  1973   "Effect of Interviewers' Sex on Interview Responses,"
          in John B. McKinlay, ed., Research Methods in Health
          Care. New York: Milbank Memorial Fund.
Edgerton, R. B.
  1967   The Cloak of Competence. Berkeley: University of
          California Press.
Farber, Bernard
  1959   "Effects of a Severely Mentally Retarded Child on
          Family Integration." Monographs of the Society for
          Research in Child Development. Series 71. Vol. 24,
          No. 2. Lafayette, Indiana: Society for Research in
          Child Development.

Goffman, Erving
    1961   Asylums. Garden City, New York: Doubleday, Anchor
            Books.
    1974   Frame Analysis. New York: Harper & Row.
Hyman, Herbert
    1954   Interviewing in Social Research. Chicago: University
            of Chicago Press.
Mayer, J. E.
    1974   "Clash in Perspective between Mental Patients and
            Staff." American Journal of Orthopsychiatry 44: 432-41.
Richardson, Stephen A., Barbara Dohrenwend, and David Klein
    1965   Interviewing: Its Forms and Functions. New York:
            Basic Books.
Saenger, Gerhard
    1960   Factors Influencing the Institutionalization of Mentally
            Retarded Individuals in New York. Albany, New York:
            State Interdepartmental Health Resources Board.
Weinstein, R. M.
    1974   "Mental Patients' Perceptions of Illness Etiology."
            American Journal of Psychiatry 131: 798-802.

QUESTIONS ASKED OF GATEWOOD RESIDENTS
AND BACKGROUND DATA GATHERED

First Interview

I. Self-image
1. How long did you live at_____? (name of state school)
2. How old are you now?
3. What did you do on your last birthday?
4. How old were you when you came to live at_____?
5. What are some of the reasons you went to live at_____?
6. When you were at_____, how did you spend your time? Tell me what you did each day. Where did you sleep? What did you do when you woke up?
7. What were some of the things you like about_____? Was it hard to leave_____?
8. What were some of the things you didn't like about_____?
9. How do you feel about being in this place?
10. Why do you think you were asked to live here?
11. What are some of the things you would like to do here?
12. Is there anything you don't want to do?
13. What are some of the things you can do?
14. Do you think you will learn to do things here? (If yes, what? If no, why not?)

II. Interpersonal Relations
15. Do you get along with other people?
16. What are some of the things about you which make it easy for you to get along with other people? What are some of things about you which make it hard for you to get along with other people?
17. Who do you know at_____?
18. If you needed help, who did you go to see?
19. Is there anyone from_____you miss? Who is that? Why do you miss him/her?
20. Is there anyone from_____you would like to bring along with you to Gatewood?
21. Who did you eat your meals with at_____?

127

22. Who did you go to the PX with at _____ ?
23. Did you have a boyfriend/girlfriend at _____ ?
24. Who did you have fun with? Who did you fool around with?
25. Did anyone ever tease you? Did you ever tease anybody?
26. Did anyone ever fight with you at _____ ? Did you ever fight with anybody?
27. Was there anyone you were afraid of at _____ ? (If yes, who?)
28. Did your people come to visit you at _____ ? (If yes, who?)
29. Did you ever go home? (If yes, when?)
30. Did you ever go off the grounds by yourself? (If yes, where did you go?)
31. Did you ever go get things for the attendants? (If yes, what?)
32. What other things did you do for the attendants?
33. What did you get for doing that?
34. What did the attendants do for you?

III. Self-care skills
35. If you were going to a party, how would you get ready?
36. What clothes would you wear for a party?
37. If you didn't have nice clothes, would you go to the party or would you stay home?
38. If you had to make breakfast for yourself, what would you do?
39. Tell me how you make those things.
40. Where would you get them from?
41. Do you know how much each thing costs?
42. Where would you get the money?
43. Could you earn the money? (If yes, how?)
44. Where would you keep the money?
45. If someone asked you for the money you had to buy things for breakfast what would you tell them? Why would you say that?

IV. Working
46. Did you work while at _____ ?
47. What did you do?
48. How did you get the job?
49. Did you want the job? (If no, did you want a different job?)
50. Did you like the job? (Why? Why not?)
51. Did you work for pay? (If yes, how much did you get?)
52. Was this enough? (Why? Why not?)
53. Did you ask for more? (If yes, what happened?)

54. Did you work alone? Did you have to be quiet when you worked?
55. Did you get the things you needed for the job?
56. Did you do a good job? How do you know you did a good job?
57. Did you have any other jobs at _____? Why did you change jobs?
58. Which job did you like better? Why?
59. Did anyone teach you how to do these jobs? (If yes, who?)
60. Did you ever teach anyone else how to do the job? (If yes, who?)
61. Did you like teaching others how to do the job? (If yes, why?) (If no, why not?)

V. Leisure time
62. Did you have any fun at _____?
63. What did you like to do? Anything else?
64. Did you do this alone or with other patients?
65. Did you get a chance to fool around? What did you do?
66. Did anyone try to stop you from doing that?
67. What happened if you were caught?
68. Did anyone ever teach you to do these things?
69. Did you ever teach other patients to do these things?
70. Can you fool around here? (Why? Why not?)
71. What things would you like to do here for fun?

VI. Decision-making
72. What time did you go to bed at _____?
73. Who decided that?
74. What happened if you wanted to stay up later?
75. What time did you wake up in the morning at _____?
76. Who decided that?
77. What happened if you wanted to stay in bed late?
78. When did you eat lunch?
79. Who decided that?
80. Did you ever know anyone who tried to change the rules? (If yes, what happened?)
81. Where did you get your clothing from? Could you wear anything you wanted?
82. Who decided when you could get a haircut/have your hair done?
83. Who decided when you needed to take a shower?

VII. Social competency
84. An aide is holding your money and you want it but he is on the telephone. What do you do?
85. A new resident moved in at Gatewood. You don't know him/her but you want to meet him/her. What do you do?
86. A resident is using your radio but he/she didn't ask if he/she could use it. What do you do?
87. An aide steps on your toe accidentally. What do you do?
88. Your roommate plays his/her radio late at night and you cannot sleep. What do you do?
89. The resident next door keeps everyone awake by playing his radio. By mistake the aide punishes you by taking away your radio. What do you do?
90. What would you do with $300.00?

Second Interview

I. Self-image
1. When did you come to live at Gatewood?
2. What are some of the reasons why you came here?
3. Why do you think you were asked to live here?
4. How do you spend your time each day? Could you tell me what you do each day? What did you do yesterday? What was the first thing you did when you woke up? Then what did you do? What did you do in the evening? What do you do on weekends?
5. What did you do on your last birthday?
6. How do you feel about being in this place?
7. What do you like the most about being here? What do you like the least?
8. Where did you live before you came here? Is it different here than at _____? (name of state school) Why? Why not?
9. What are some of the things you want to do here?
10. Have you been able to do those things?
11. Are there any things you don't want to do? If yes, what are they?
12. Are there any things around here which are hard to get used to? If yes, what?
13. What are some of the things you can do?
14. Did you learn to do any of those things here? (If yes, what? If no, why not?)

II. Interpersonal relations

15. Do you get along with other people?
16. What are some of the things about you which make it easy for you to get along with other people? What are some of the things about you which make it hard for you to get along with other people?
17. Who do you know here? (If names are given, get respondent to identify them.)
18. If you need help who do you go to see?
19. Is there anyone who helps you every so often? If yes, who is it?
20. Is there anyone who you help every so often? If yes, who is it?
21. Who do you eat your meals with here? Do you eat with anybody special? (If names are given, get respondent to identify them.)
22. Do you go to the store with anybody? (If yes, who is it?)
23. Do you have a boyfriend/girlfriend now? Where do you meet him/her? If yes, who?
24. Who do you fool around with? (Identify)
25. Does anyone ever tease you here? If yes, who is that? (Identify)
26. Do you ever tease anybody? If yes, who is that? (Identify)
27. Do you ever fight with anybody? If yes, who is that? (Identify)
28. Do your people come visit you here? If yes, who?
29. Do you ever go visit your people? If yes, who?
30. Do you ever go home with other residents? If yes, who?
31. Do you ever visit anyone else? If yes, who is it?
32. Does anyone else ever visit you? If yes, who is it?
33. Do you ever go for a walk with anybody? If yes, who is it? If yes, where do you go?
34. Do you ever go for a walk alone? If yes, where do you go? If no, why not?
35. Do you ever go get things for the aides? If yes, what? What do you get for it?
36. What other things do you do for aides?
37. What do the aides do for you?

III. Self-care skills

38. If you were going to a party, how would you get ready?
39. What clothes would you wear for a party?
40. If you didn't have nice clothes would you go to the party or would you stay home? Why would you do that?

41. If you had to make breakfast for yourself, what would you do?
42. Tell me how you make those things.
43. Where would you get them from?
44. Do you know how much each thing costs?
45. Where would you get the money?
46. Could you earn the money? If yes, how?
47. Where would you keep the money?
48. If someone asked you for the money you had to buy things for breakfast, what would you tell them? Why would you say that?

IV. Working
49. Do you work?
50. What do you do?
51. How did you get the job?
52. Did you want that job? If no, did you want a different job?
53. Do you like the job? Why not?
54. Do you work for pay? If yes, how much do you get?
55. Is this enough? Why? Why not?
56. Did you ask for more? (If yes, what happened?)
57. Do you work alone or with someone else? Do you have to be quiet when you work?
58. Do you eat lunch with other people from work or by yourself? If yes, with anyone special?
59. Do you get the things you need for the job at work?
60. Do you do a good job? How do you know you do a good job?
61. Did you have any other jobs before this one? If yes, why did you change jobs?
62. Which job do you like better? Why?
63. Did anyone teach you how to do these jobs? If yes, who?
64. Did you ever teach anyone else how to do a job? If yes, who?
65. Did you like teaching others how to do a job? If yes, why? If no, why not?

V. Leisure time
Now I would like to talk to you about what you do when you have free time.
66. Do you have any fun here? If no, why not?
67. What do you like to do? Anything else?
68. Do you do this alone or with other people? If with others, with whom? (Identify)
69. Do you get a chance to fool around? What do you do? If yes, with whom?

70. Does anyone try to stop you from doing that? If yes, who?
71. What happens if you are caught?
72. Did anyone ever teach you to do these things? If yes, who?
73. Did you ever teach other residents to do these things? If yes, who?

VI. Decision-making
Let me ask you something about living here.
74. What time do you go to bed?
75. Who decides that?
76. What happens if you want to stay up later?
77. What time do you wake up in the morning?
78. Who decides that?
79. What happens if you want to stay in bed late?
80. Did you ever know anyone who tried to change the rules here? (If yes, what happened?)
81. Who decides when you could get a haircut here/have your hair done?
82. Who decides when you need to take a shower?
83. Who decides when to wash your clothes?

VII. Social competency
Now let me ask you some other things about living here.
84. Suppose an aide is holding your money and you want it but he is on the telephone. What do you do?
85. Suppose a new resident moves in at Gatewood. You don't know him/her but you want to meet him/her. What do you do?
86. Suppose a resident is using your radio but he/she didn't ask if he could use it. What do you do?
87. Suppose an aide steps on your toe accidentally. What do you do?
88. Suppose your roommate plays his/her radio late at night and you cannot sleep. What do you do?
89. Suppose the resident next door keeps everyone awake by playing his radio. By mistake, the aide punishes you by taking away your radio. What do you do?
90. What would you do with $300.00?

Third Interview

I. Self-image
Now that you have been living at Gatewood for some time, I would like to ask you about your experiences.

1. First, tell me what are some of the reasons why you came to live here?
2. Many people here have told me what they do every day. What is the first thing you do when you wake up? Then what do you do? What do you do in the evening? What do you do on weekends?
3. What did you do on your last birthday?
4. How do you feel about being in this place?
5. What are some of the things you like most about being here?
6. Is there anything you don't like about being here?
7. Are there any things around here which are hard to get used to? If yes, what?
8. What are some of the things you would like to do here when you are older?
9. Are there any things you don't want to do? What are they?
10. What are some of the things you are able to do?
11. If you had to make breakfast for yourself, what would you do?
12. Tell me how you make those things.
13. Where would you get them from?
14. Do you know how much each thing costs?
15. Where would you get the money?
16. Could you earn the money?

II. Interpersonal relations
17. Who do you know at Gatewood?
18. Who do you eat your meals with at Gatewood?
19. Do you ever go to visit your people?
20. Who do you visit? Do you go along or do they come and get you?
21. Do you ever visit anyone else? (If yes, who is it?)
22. Does anyone else ever visit you? (If yes, who is it?)
23. Do you ever go for a walk with anybody? (If yes, who is it?)
24. Where do you go?
25. Do you go to the store with anybody? (If yes, who is it?)
26. Do you have a boyfriend/girlfriend now?
27. Who is your boyfriend/girlfriend?
28. Where did you meet him/her?
29. Who do you fool around with?
30. Does anyone ever tease you?
31. Do you ever tease anyone?
32. Do your people come to visit you at Gatewood?
33. Who came to visit you?

34. What do the aides do for you?
35. Some people go for help to people they know on the outside.
    Do you go for help to anyone on the outside?
36. Who is that?
37. Anyone else?

III. Self-care skills
38. Since you came to live here have you ever gone to a
    (see list below)?
39. a. Were any staff with you? b. Were any other residents
    with you?

a. Ball game	d. Parents
b. Museum	e. Friend's house
c. Zoo	f. Outside party
d. Outside movie	g. Restaurant
e. Park	h. Church or synagogue
f. Community center	i. Bar
g. Store	j. Any other place (Specify)

40. On a day off do you ever go places?
41. Where did you go?
42. How did you get there?
43. Did you do this with anyone else?
44. Who did you do this with?
45. Who is this person?
46. What did you do on last Saturday and Sunday?
47. Would you like to go somewhere else?
48. Where would you like to go?
49. Have you ever been to these places?
50. Now let me ask you a few questions about this place. Do
    you know the name of the street Gatewood is on?
51. What do you call this neighborhood?
52. What do you call this part of the city?

IV. Working
53. Do you work?
54. What do you do?
55. Did you go to work yesterday?
56. Did you go to work with anyone else?
57. Who did you go with?
58. How did you get to work?
59. Do you get a break when you work?
60. What do you do on your breaks?

61. Do you eat lunch where you work?
62. Do you eat lunch with anybody?
63. Who do you eat lunch with?
64. Who is this person?
65. After lunch do you go for a walk with anyone?
66. Who did you go with?
67. While you work, do you talk to anybody?
68. Who do you talk to?

V. Leisure time
69. Do you have fun here?
70. What do you like to do?
71. Do you do this alone or with other people? (If with others, with whom?)

VI. Decision-making
72. Who decides what time you go to bed?
73. What happens if you want to stay up late?
74. Who decides what time you wake up in the morning?
75. Who decides when you should get a haircut here or have your hair done?
76. Who decides when you need to take a shower?
77. Who decides when to wash your clothes?
78. Do you wash your own clothes?
79. Are you allowed to use the washing machine?

VII. Social competency
80. Suppose an aide is holding your money and you want it but he is on the telephone. What do you do?
81. Suppose a new resident moves in at Gatewood. You don't know him/her but you want to meet him/her. What do you do?
82. Suppose a resident is using your radio but he/she didn't ask if he could use it. What do you do?
83. Suppose an aide steps on your toe accidentally. What do you do?
84. Suppose your roommate plays his/her radio late at night and you cannot sleep. What do you do?
85. Suppose the resident next door keeps everyone awake by playing his/her radio. By mistake, the aide punishes you by taking away your radio. What do you do?
86. What would you do with $300.00?

Background Data

1. Sex
2. Ethnicity
3. Date of Birth
4. Date of admission to state school
5. Date of transfer from state school
6. Length of stay at state school
7. Prior institutionalization
8. I.Q. scores: date, name of test, score
9. Education
10. Medical problems
11. Medication upon transfer
12. Behavior in year prior to transfer
13. Family history
14. Daily activity since eighteenth birthday

ARNOLD BIRENBAUM, Ph.D., is a sociologist who has published extensively in the area of health care and disability. His research on social aspects of mental retardation include studies of the adaptations of mothers of mentally retarded children, an evaluation of the innovation and stabilization of a recreational program in the community, and a survey of the employment status of retarded adults. He is editor of Health and Medicine, Intellect: A Review of Professional Thought. Dr. Birenbaum is Assistant Professor of Psychiatry and Community Health, Albert Einstein College of Medicine, Yeshiva University, where he is now engaged in research in community mental health. At the State University of New York, College at Purchase, he is Adjunct Associate Professor of Sociology.

SAMUEL SEIFFER is a doctoral candidate in the department of sociology at Columbia University. His principle interest is the relationship between bureaucracies and family groups. He has taught at the City College of New York, Kingsborough College, New York, and the College of New Rochelle. The author of several delivered papers, his work has also appeared in Contemporary Sociology and Sociological Analysis.

ACCOUNTABILITY IN HEALTH FACILITIES
Harry I. Greenfield
epilogue by Amitai Etzioni

BEHAVIORAL SCIENCE TECHNIQUES: An
Annotated Bibliography for Health Professionals
Monique K. Tichy

MENTAL HEALTH AND RETARDATION
POLITICS: The Mind Lobbies in Congress
Daniel A. Felicetti